IMAGES
of America

MISSION

Plaques on the facade of La Lomita Mission, shown in this undated photograph, attest to the chapel's importance as a Recorded Texas Historic Landmark (1964). Additional honors include the National Register of Historic Places (1975) and National Register Historic District (1981). The octagonal marker commemorates the Oblate Missionary Trail. In 2008, the City of Mission funded renovations to the chapel, which was built of local materials in 1899. (Courtesy Mission Historical Museum.)

ON THE COVER: Partners John J. Conway and James W. Hoit founded Mission, Texas, in 1908. Conway (far right, seated) and members of his family are shown here on the porch of the Mission Hotel in January 1909. Statesman William Jennings Bryan (center, seated next to the porch post) bought land and built a home in Mission. Although Hoit disappeared under mysterious circumstances, Conway remained and is acknowledged as the founder of Mission. (Courtesy Mission Historical Museum.)

IMAGES
of America

MISSION

Karen Gerhardt Fort and the
Mission Historical Museum, Inc.

ARCADIA
PUBLISHING

Published by Arcadia Publishing
Charleston, South Carolina

Library of Congress Control Number: 2009920422

For all general information contact Arcadia Publishing at:
Telephone 843-853-2070
Fax 843-853-0044
E-mail sales@arcadiapublishing.com
For customer service and orders:
Toll-Free 1-888-313-2665

Visit us on the Internet at www.arcadiapublishing.com

*Dedicated to the memory of John J. Conway and
to the residents of the city he loved.*

CONTENTS

ACKNOWLEDGMENTS

The author is indebted to many individuals for their time and expertise in the preparation of this book. Adela Ortega, director of the Mission Historical Museum, Inc., expressed enthusiasm for the project and made available the time of her staff as well as the photograph archives belonging to the museum. Without her support, this book would not have been possible. Staff members Maria Picazo and Adrian Garza devoted many hours to the success of the book. Picazo located photographs and conducted research, while Garza scanned the images with skill and patience. Patti Golden Burrows, Angela Lopez, Felix Gutierrez, and Linda Castañeda provided vital support throughout the project. Vernon G. Weckbacher joined the museum after the research and scanning were underway, and his skill as an archivist proved invaluable. Salomón and Blanca Marroquín, Fr. Roy Snipes of Our Lady of Guadalupe Catholic Church, and Sylvia Moralez of St. Paul's Catholic Church provided historical details and context. Carlos B. De la Garza clarified many important points in a lengthy interview. Judy Sailer, of McAllen's Miller International Airport; Rosalba Martinez, in the office of Ismael "Kino" Flores; and Eligio "Kika" and Lucille De la Garza provided critically helpful details.

The author is eager to thank Mathew Martin, archivist at the Southwestern Oblate Historical Archives, Oblate School of Theology, in San Antonio, Texas, for permission to use photographs in chapter one and for reviewing the introduction and captions for accuracy.

The author is deeply grateful to Scott and Mary Alice Martin, who generously shared information, stories, photographs, documents, and family history. Mary Alice Martin is the granddaughter of John Conway and the daughter of Roy Conway. She clarified many points of puzzlement due to contradictory or missing information, and her memories lifted the Conways out of photographs and brought them to life as real people. The Martins' beautiful garden is a tribute to the pioneers who left their long-familiar homes to settle in the Lower Rio Grande Valley and to build the City of Mission.

I wish to thank Kristie Kelly of Arcadia Publishing for her guidance, assistance, and cheerleading, initially as acquisitions editor and now as publisher. As we say in South Texas, "¡Viva, Kristie!"

Unless otherwise noted, all images appear courtesy of the Mission Historical Museum, Inc.

INTRODUCTION

Mission, Texas, is named for the small chapel on the Rio Grande south of the present city. Between 1748 and 1753, Spanish settlers recruited by Gov. José de Escandón (1700–1770) from what is now northern Mexico occupied the land along the Río Bravo del Norte (known in the United States as the Rio Grande). Beginning in 1749, the settlers raised livestock, grew vegetables, and built small towns, but they did not receive formal grants of land ownership from the Spanish government until 1767. At that time, the settlers' claims were divided into *porciones* (portions), blocks of land measuring nine-thirteenths of a mile wide and extending from 11 to 16 miles inland. Each *porción* began at the river to ensure access to water. Over time, through purchase by different owners, the ranch property that later included the chapel occupied *porciones* 55, 56, and 57. The city of Mission crosses eight *porciones* (53–60). Thus, the history of Mission is deeply rooted in the soil of Spanish Texas.

The U.S. war with Mexico (1846–1848) brought many American soldiers through South Texas, and some returned after the war. They settled in towns along the river and often bought large tracts of land. However, limited water supply discouraged large-scale agriculture, and land use remained dedicated to ranching.

Reynosa merchant René Guillard bought *porción* 57 from the widow of John (Juan) Davis Bradburn (1787–1842) in 1845. Bradburn, a Virginian with Mexican citizenship who was the customs inspector at Anáhuac during the Battle of Velasco and who fought at the Battle of San Jacinto in 1836, had purchased the ranch in 1842. He is believed to be buried on the property. Guillard bought *porción* 55 in 1851. The two ranches, totaling more than 10,000 acres, employed numerous workers and their families.

The first priests known as the Oblates of Mary Immaculate arrived at Point Isabel in 1849 and began their missionary work in Brownsville. In 1852, they expanded their ministry to the faithful living on ranches and farms along the Rio Grande, and by 1867, their territory reached Roma, about 100 miles upriver from Brownsville. These hardy priests, who labored so diligently in the harsh environment of the brush country, were known as the Cavalry of Christ.

René Guillard's ranch at La Lomita, about halfway between Roma and Brownsville, became a place for the missionaries to visit with each other and to rest during their travels. A Roman Catholic, Guillard built a small chapel where the Oblate Fathers offered religious services to ranch employees and their families. In his 1861 will, Guillard bequeathed his two ranch properties (La Lomita and El Nogalito) to Fr. Pierre F. Parisot and Fr. Pierre Y. Keralum. The property was formally transferred to the Missionary Society of Oblate Fathers of Texas in 1877.

In 1883, the Oblate Fathers purchased the middle section (*porción* 56) of over 5,700 acres, thus combining the property for more efficient management. Altogether the entire land grant of three *porciones*, called La Lomita ("little hill"), occupied 2 miles along the river and 15 miles inland. The missionaries began ranching and farming in 1884, but with marginal success.

In 1899, the Oblate Fathers established a mission district to serve the 65 ranches of Hidalgo County, with headquarters at La Lomita. Although there had been a small chapel on René

Guillard's ranch property, the one built in 1899 (just inside *porción* 56) is the structure known today. Oblate records indicate that Fr. Francis Bugnard, O.M.I., with Fr. René Pescheur and two lay brothers, built the chapel and the brick rectory. The chapel walls were filled with stones from the hill about a half-mile away. A small community grew up around the chapel.

By January 1906, when James W. Hoit and John J. Conway arrived in the Rio Grande Valley, the Oblate Fathers were having difficulty making enough income to offset expenses. They were willing to sell some of their land. Hoit, a Minneapolis grain merchant, and Wisconsin native John J. Conway, who had been developing land in South Dakota but had recently moved to Minneapolis, recognized the potential for small farms and the need for a nearby market town.

In 1907, after five days of tough negotiations with Fr. Henri Ambrose Constantineau, the Oblate provincial in San Antonio, Conway and Hoit purchased 17,000 acres of La Lomita. The Oblates retained about 400 acres, some along the Rio Grande, including the chapel, and some in the proposed townsite. (Conway and Hoit deeded Block 104 and Block 105, lots 1 through 6, to the Oblates for a church.) Conway and Hoit added another 10,000 acres bought from James B. Wells and John Closner for a total of 27,000 acres.

Conway and Hoit opened an office near La Lomita and formed the Mission Land Improvement Company, Inc. In July 1907, they hired surveyor Sidney J. Rowe to subdivide the land into 40-acre tracts for small farms. The following month, their new Mission Canal Company began construction of irrigation canals and the first of three pumping plants to provide farms with water from the Rio Grande. During the 1950s, after a new pumping plant was built, Mission converted the property to recreational use, known today as Chimney Park.

In February 1908, Conway and four partners set up the Lomita Cooperative Irrigation Company to sell water to landowners at $1 per acre. Conway and Hoit advertised throughout the Midwest, and parties of "land seekers" came by train to inspect the area for themselves. The first tracts sold for $35 to $60 per acre. (Later tracts would sell for $100 to $125 per acre.) According to a promotional brochure printed in 1911, within three years, 15,000 acres had been sold and 10,000 acres were in productive cultivation.

Conway, Hoit, and newcomers Charles and Rose Volz chose "Mission" as the name for their stop on the branch line of the St. Louis, Brownsville, and Mexico Railway. The depot, with its passenger, freight, and telegraph station, opened on December 15, 1908. According to the 1911 brochure, Mission's only two buildings at that time were the depot and a restaurant. A post office, hotel, general store, and lumber yard sprang up almost over night. Mission was formally dedicated on February 23, 1909, and by August, a grid of 13 streets east and west and 13 streets north and south comprised the town. Lomita Boulevard, the main street, extended north and south. The fast-growing town was incorporated on December 9, 1910.

The promised sale of water at $1 per acre proved impractical, forcing the Lomita Cooperative Irrigation Company into receivership by 1912. Although James Hoit disappeared from Mission, Conway remained, serving on the board of the First State Bank of Mission and developing other properties, until his death in 1931 at the age of 71.

During the past 100 years, Mission has become known for its excellent grapefruit; colorful citrus fiesta celebration; superb military tradition; and abundance of national leaders in agriculture, politics, sports, and literature. We hope the reader will be delighted—and surprised—at the remarkable history of this charming city.

One

THE CHAPEL
AT LA LOMITA

Most ranch families in the Lower Rio Grande Valley lived in jacales. A typical jacal, shown in this undated photograph, consisted of stout tree limbs placed upright in the ground to support a roof beam; smaller branches used as lathes to form the walls; a covering of mud or plaster; and a thatched roof. These ancient construction methods and materials have been found in the walls of La Lomita Chapel.

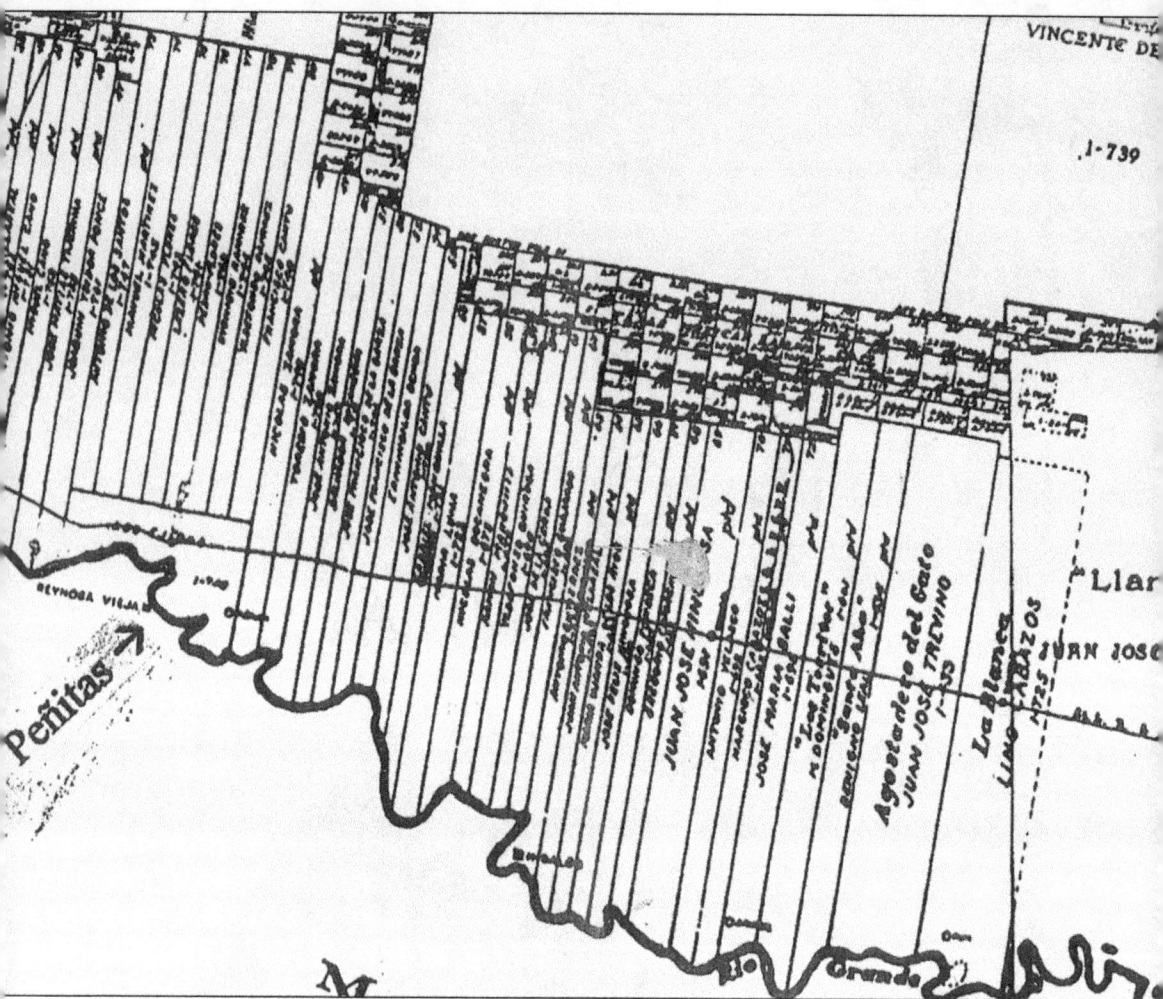

This 1911 map from the Texas General Land Office shows the *porciones* granted by the King of Spain in 1767. *Porción* numbering began at Laredo and continued downstream along the Rio Grande to Brownsville. *Porciones* measured nine-thirteenths of a mile wide and up to 16 miles inland on both sides of the Rio Grande. Each *porción* began at the river to ensure access to water. The ranch and later the mission that became known as La Lomita ("little hill") included *porciones* 55, 56, and 57. Mission occupies eight *porciones* (53–60). Major north-south thoroughfares such as Bentsen Road, Stewart Road, Los Ebanos Road, Inspiration Road, Moore Field Road, and Lahoma Road identify *porción* boundaries.

In 1899, La Lomita Ranch became the headquarters for the new Oblate Mission District. This c. 1910 photograph shows the southwest corner of the chapel. The adjacent building had a guest room for visitors, a room for a lay brother who worked as a handyman, and a room for supplies, which were sold to the ranch families. The original mud-and-lathe walls have been covered with planks. (Courtesy Southwestern Oblate Historical Archives, Oblate School of Theology, San Antonio, Texas.)

Mission buildings, shown here around 1912, were laid out around a central plaza and included the rectory (far left, indicated by the porch roof), a ranch house (center left), storehouse and guest quarters (center right), and the chapel (far right, seen here from the southeast corner). Wagon sheds and a blacksmith shop stood nearby. An unpaved street, wide enough for wagons, separated the plaza from the homes of ranch workers. (Courtesy Southwestern Oblate Historical Archives, Oblate School of Theology, San Antonio, Texas.)

Soon after building the chapel, called Our Lady of the Mission, the Oblate Fathers constructed this brick rectory, consisting of five rooms and a shaded porch, on the south side of the plaza. Because five priests were seldom in residence at the same time, one room became a recreation room for visiting and playing chess. This view shows roof repairs made in 1935. (Courtesy Southwestern Oblate Historical Archives, Oblate School of Theology, San Antonio, Texas.)

In 1910, the Oblate Fathers built a new church and rectory in Mission, dedicated on January 20, 1911. This 1911 photograph taken near the new church shows Fathers Paul E. Hally, Jules A. Bornes, Jean Horeau, Henri M. Janvier, Jean-Baptiste Bretault (usually known as "Juan de la Costa"), Francois Bugnard, and Eugene Regent. The brick chimney from the first pump station, built in 1907, stands in the background. (Courtesy Southwestern Oblate Historical Archives, Oblate School of Theology, San Antonio, Texas.)

In 1912, the Oblate Fathers built St. Peter's Novitiate, a retreat for prospective priests, on La Lomita Hill about a half-mile from the chapel. The Oblates left in 1972, and the building served as a mental health facility until September 6, 2009, when it was damaged by fire. This view is prior to the fire. (Courtesy Tom A. Fort, 2009.)

This modest entrance welcomes visitors to La Lomita Mission and park grounds. A brick pathway invites visitors to explore the chapel and the original plaza. A statue of Mary Immaculate identifies the location of the rectory. Parking is plentiful, picnic tables and restrooms are available, and admission is free. (Courtesy Tom A. Fort, 2009.)

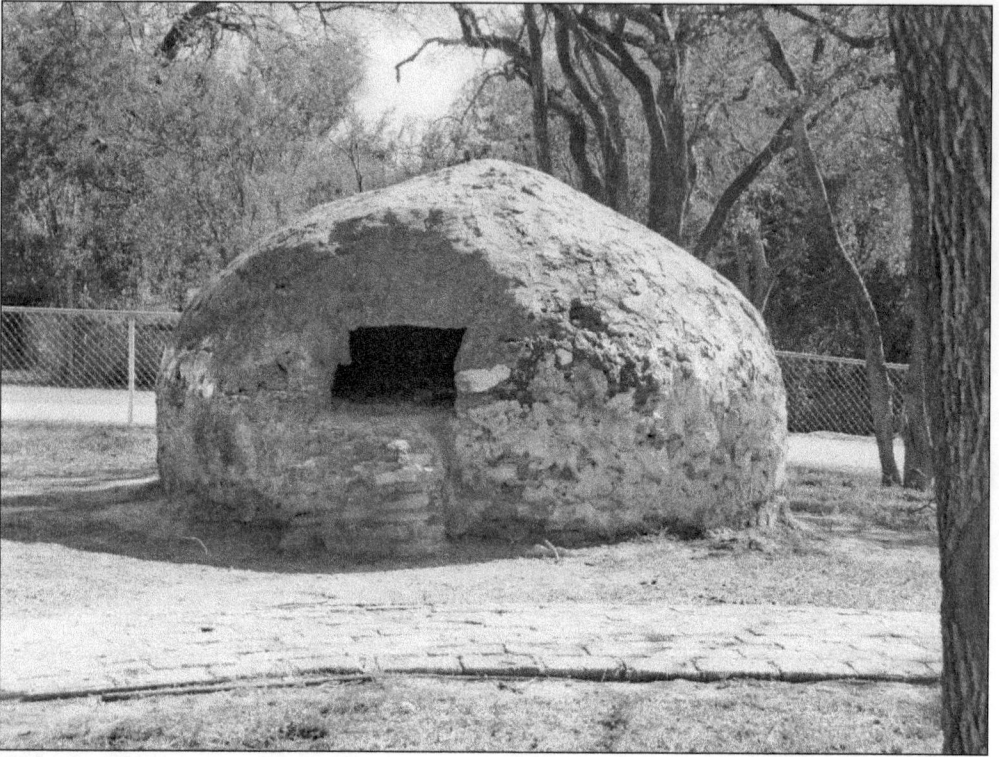

Today the guest quarters and storehouse, ranch house, jacales, wagon sheds, blacksmith shop, and rectory are gone, but two ancillary structures, an oven and a well, remain. The large outdoor oven (*horno*), shaped like a beehive, stands in the southwest corner of the grounds. (Courtesy Tom A. Fort, 2009.)

The mission well, without the windmill, is a feature of the picnic area. In the distance beyond the chapel stands a levee, part of the border wall system built by the U.S. Department of Homeland Security in 2008. Visitors cross the levee to enter the park. Open fields and the seminary are visible from the top of the levee. (Courtesy Tom A. Fort, 2009.)

The chapel has been restored several times, first in 1912. In 1928, Fr. Isidore P. Chateau, writing from La Lomita, described repairs such as the replacement of roof shingles and attachment of new ceiling canvas. Further restoration by the residents of nearby Madero took place in 1939, after the hurricane of 1933 caused extensive damage. Another restoration and development of the park grounds followed in 1976 as a U.S. Bicentennial project. (Courtesy Tom A. Fort, 2009.)

The Diocese of Brownsville bought the property from the Oblate Fathers in 1999. To commemorate the city's centennial, the City of Mission contracted with Kell Muñoz Architects of San Antonio and the 5125 Company of Mission to complete a new restoration. After six months of effort and a cost of over $200,000, the chapel was restored and rededicated in 2008. (Courtesy Tom A. Fort, 2009.)

Two

JOHN J. CONWAY AND THE FOUNDING OF MISSION

To attract the St. Louis, Brownsville, and Mexico Railway to his new townsite, John J. Conway arranged to build a depot at his own expense, grade the land, provide the ties for a siding, and give the railroad 20 acres of land. In return, the railroad installed the tracks and named the stop "Mission." This image shows the depot around 1909.

John J. Conway (1860–1931) was the son of Patrick (?–1902) and Bridget (1833–1925) Conway, who came to America from Ireland in 1854. After a year in New York, they settled in Rudolph, Wood County, Wisconsin, where John Conway was born. He moved to Orient, Faulk County, South Dakota, in 1883, where he owned a farm and a store called Conway Brothers, which he later operated with his older brother Martin. In 1887, John Conway became the first postmaster of Orient, housing the post office in the store, which also featured the town's first telephone office. John Conway married Elizabeth Henafin, and they had four children: Helen "Nellie" (1886–1944), Roy (1889–1959), and twins Maurine (1892–1976) and Myron "Mike" (1892–1946). Nellie, a physician, lived in California near her sister, Maurine Conway Murray. Roy joined his father in Mission. Mike enlisted in the U.S. Army, achieved the rank of colonel, and served on the staff of Gen. Douglas MacArthur. This photograph of John Conway dates from around 1911.

When Elizabeth died in 1898, John Conway, who was Roman Catholic, placed the children in a convent. He soon married Emma Dowling of Detroit, Michigan, shown in this undated photograph, and reunited his family. Two children were born to John and Emma Conway: John H. in 1906 and William E. in 1908. Emma divided her time between Mission and Minneapolis, and John traveled back and forth to be with her.

John Conway began selling land near Orient, South Dakota, around 1900. This undated business card shows his primary office to be in Minneapolis, with two branch offices in Faulkton and Orient. After graduation from high school, Roy Conway opened a land office for John at Faulkton and joined the Mission Land Improvement Company in 1908.

Roy Patrick Conway, examining a cluster of grapes, was both a real estate agent and assistant superintendent of the Mission Canal Company. He bought three lots from his father on December 6, 1909, at a cost of $1,000. The property, purchased for resale, occupied the corner of Cedar Street and Lomita Boulevard.

IRRIGATED LANDS

the head of the irrigation strict of the Lower Rio 'ande. Eighty miles of nal built and three pump-s plants in operation hav-g a total capacity of 150,-oo gallons discharge per Minute

Mission Land Improvement Company.

WE PROVE IT

Water for irrigation unlimited Every farm is under the ditch Prices and terms reasonable. Returns from yields great Opportunities unexcelled Values rapidly increasing Every month a harvest time Ideal climate, fertile soil Temperature mild, equable

JOHN J. CONWAY
PRESIDENT AND OWNER

ROY P. CONWAY,
SECRETARY-TREASURER

The most Progressive, Highly Developed, Prosperous and Thriving Proposition in the Lower Rio Grande Valley

This letterhead from Mission Land Improvement Company, naming John J. Conway as president-owner and Roy P. Conway as secretary-treasurer, promotes the success of Mission farms through "eighty miles of canals" and "three pumping plants" with a "total capacity of 150,000 gallons of discharge per minute." Because of irrigation, the mild climate, and fertile soil, each month, Conway claimed, was "a harvest time." Conway's slogan was, "We Prove It."

Photographed at the Mission Hotel in January 1909 are, from left to right, the following: (first row, seated on stairs) C. W. Frick and Nellie Conway; (second row, standing left of post) Will McShane, Milton Kennedy, and Maurine Conway; (second row, seated on stairs) William Jennings Bryan, Emma Conway holding son John, Mary Bryan, and John J. Conway; (third row, standing far left) Mrs. Thomas Burton and Mr. Burton; (third row, standing on stairs) Mrs. J. S. McGlaughlin, ? Walker, Roy Conway, Judge Duval West; (fourth row, top of stairs) unidentified but possibly Mike Conway. William McShane (1874–1968) arrived from South Dakota, where he had known John Conway, in 1908. He settled near La Lomita Chapel, and prospective land buyers were often entertained at his home. He served as a postmaster at La Lomita, owned a tire repair shop in Mission, kept bees, and sponsored Boy Scouts. C. W. Frick worked for Conway and Hoit. He briefly served as postmaster of Mission and, in 1912, as a city commissioner. Attorney William Jennings Bryan (1860–1925) bought land from Conway and Hoit in 1909 and built a winter home in Mission in 1910.

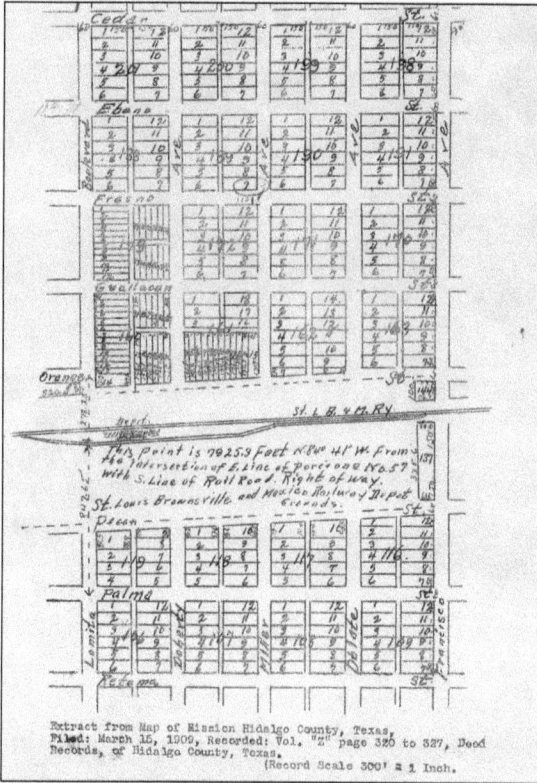

Extract from Map of Mission Hidalgo County, Texas.
Filed: March 15, 1909, Recorded: Vol. "Z" page 320 to 327, Deed
Records, of Hidalgo County, Texas.
(Record Scale 300' ± 1 Inch.

Conway and Hoit laid out the town of Mission with alleys (for trash pickup), schools, churches, a library, and residences. Lomita Boulevard, the main north-south street, was renamed Conway Boulevard in 1935. Note the location of the railroad depot and siding. This plat map was filed in the deed records of Hidalgo County on March 15, 1909. U.S. Business Highway 83 now runs parallel to the railroad tracks. By 1911, Mission boasted "three lumber yards, two cotton gins, a cotton seed oil mill, one canning factory, one bottling works, one grist mill, one bakery, two drug stores, two furniture stores, two hardware stores, two gents' furnishing stores, four general merchandise stores, three feed and grain stores, blacksmith shop, tin shop . . . and many other small business firms," according to a promotional brochure.

Railroad employees R. R. Stephens and Leo H. Marcell (both in white shirts, right of center) are helping to nudge longhorn cattle into railroad cars at Mission about 1911. In the days before fencing, Spanish cattle mixed with English cattle to produce the tough, disease-resistant longhorn, ideally suited for the brush country. Longhorns generated South Texas folklore, and the vaqueros who worked them inspired the American cowboy icon.

Addressed by R. R. Stephens to his wife on April 28, 1910, this postcard shows the Mission business district. One night, a spark in the projection room set the movie theater (far left) ablaze. The viewers evacuated, saving the piano, which was needed for silent films, and everyone ran to the Drummond Furniture Store to save the merchandise. The theater was rebuilt, and the Drummonds remained in business at another location.

The West Side Café, shown here around 1909, was an early Mission business. According to a 1911 promotional brochure advertising the Mission Land Improvement Company, the first buildings in Mission were the railroad depot and a restaurant. By 1911, there were two hotels, six restaurants, two schools, four churches, a newspaper, and an office building. Mission streets were first graded and sidewalks constructed in 1911.

Clearing crews from Texas and Mexico used machetes to hack away dense brush, cactus, and mesquite trees to prepare the land for crops. Heat, thorns, and rattlesnakes made the work

dangerous. Workers were paid 25¢ per day, the standard rate at the time. Will McShane (far right, mounted on horse and wearing large hat) was in charge of this crew around 1908.

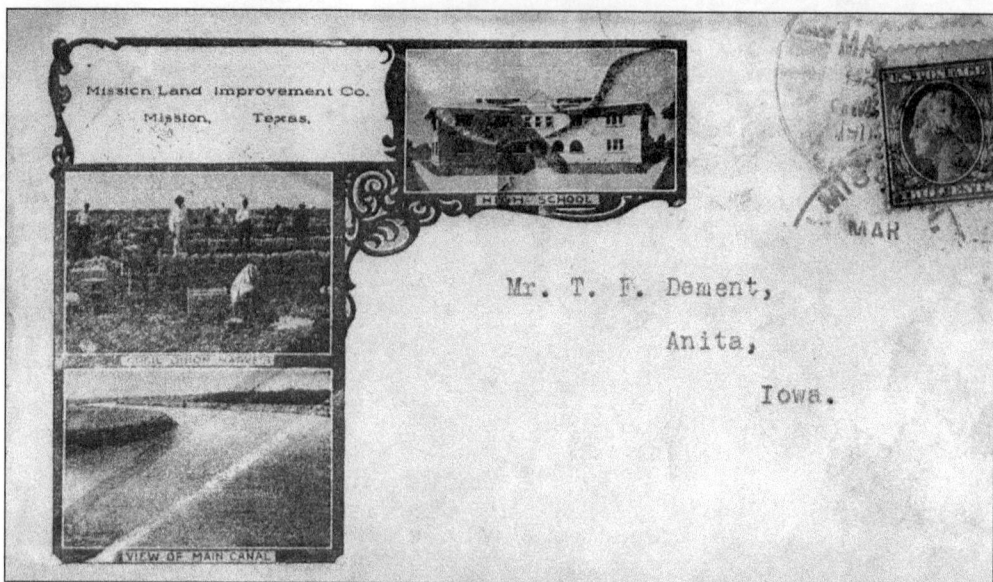

This Mission Land Improvement Company envelope, postmarked March 1911, features images of Mission High School (top, center), an onion harvest in April (left side, center), and the main irrigation canal (left side, bottom). An excursion party from Anita, Iowa, visited Mission in September 1910. The addressee was most likely a prospective land buyer.

Conway and Hoit advertised throughout the Midwest to attract farmers and their families to Mission. Many came to see the land for themselves. The weary travelers were housed at the Mission Hotel, fed well, and driven to showplace farms to convince them to move to the valley. This undated photograph shows sales agents waiting at the depot to meet an excursion train full of home seekers.

By January 6, 1912, as shown in this view of the Mission Hotel, another hotel or boardinghouse stood nearby. Conway and Hoit's business offices occupied the second floor of the brick building adjacent to the hotel (out of sight on the right). These well-dressed ladies and small boy are prospective valley settlers.

In 1907, the Mission Land and Irrigation Company hired Albert Sammons to construct irrigation canals. Laborers, hand digging the canals, earned 40¢ per day. Conway and four partners formed the Mission Canal Company to provide water to farmers at a cost of $1 per acre. In this undated photograph, Conway (center, wearing a bow tie, hat, and closed suit jacket) is showing visitors a new farmstead.

This panorama photograph, printed on the back cover of the promotional brochure, shows the Mission business district in 1911. The First State Bank of Mission stands prominently in the center (brick building), just north of the railroad depot. Facing the park are, from left to right,

a hotel or boardinghouse, the Mission Hotel, and the Mission Canal Company office building, where the Mission Historical Museum stands today on Doherty Avenue.

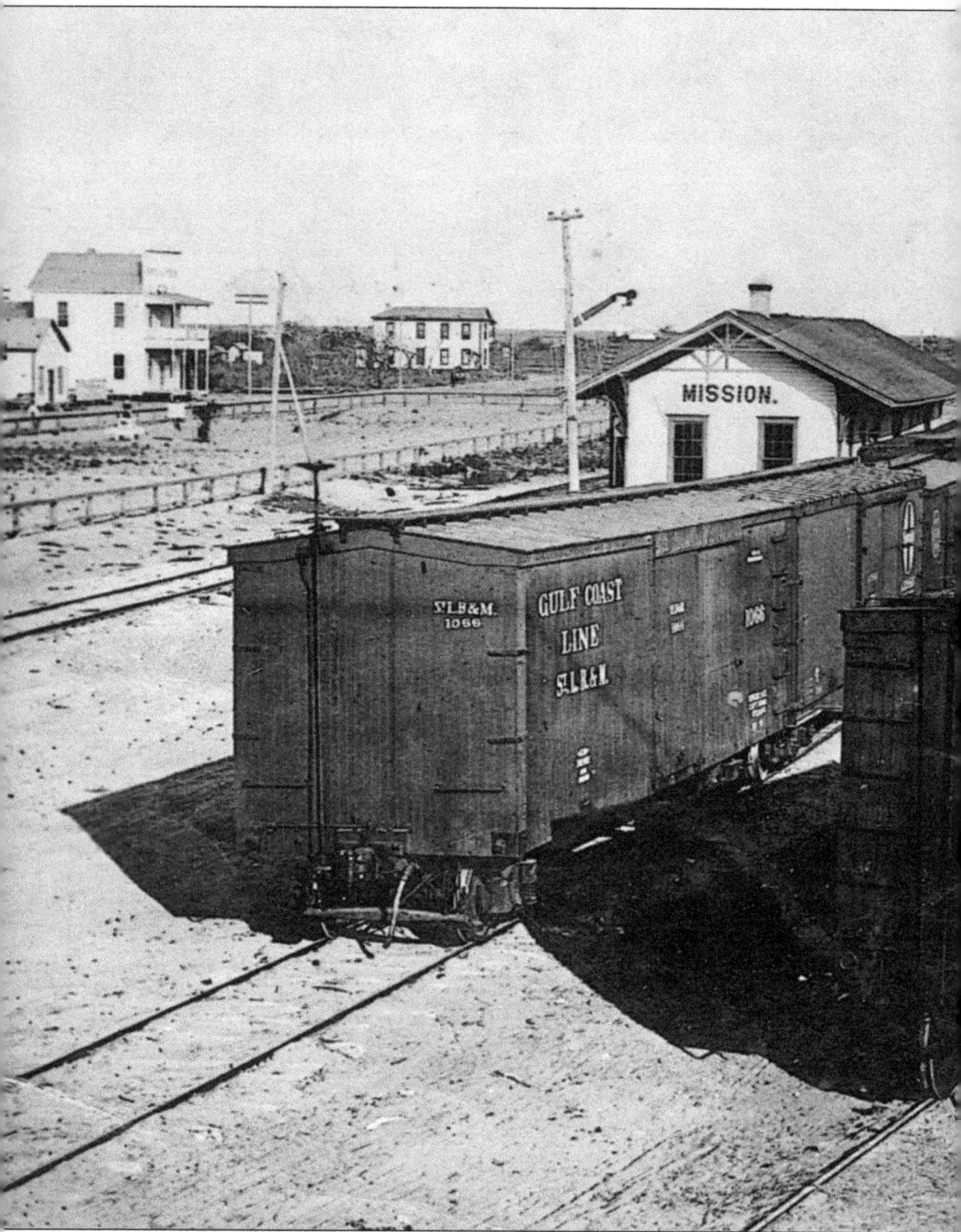

Boxcars waiting on the tracks at Mission, around 1911, delivered greatly needed building supplies. Officers of the Frisco and Rock Island Railroad lines purchased land in Mission. Note the park

and businesses (far left) and residences (far right). Cattle pens are visible just beyond the last building on the left. Acres of undeveloped land and the rail lines stretch eastward.

The A. P. Wright family moved to Mission from Cameron County during the summer of 1909. Wright had operated an experimental farm there beginning in 1906. Convinced by Conway and Hoit to relocate, Wright purchased land near La Lomita as well as in Mission. He sold nursery stock and planted many trees in town and the palms at the Shary Club House. This undated image shows the Wright nursery.

Ewell A. Wright, a son of A. P. Wright, planted extensive vegetable crops and citrus groves near La Lomita. This three-year-old lemon tree produced one bushel of lemons in 1914, the date of this photograph. E. A. and his brother, Charles P., were highly successful farmers. E. A. Wright is standing in front of the tree.

Because Mission and the surrounding farmland are higher in elevation than the Rio Grande, the company began construction of the first lift station on the river in 1907, completed in 1908, to pump water to canals and laterals. The steam-powered pumps required wood for the boiler, and a 106-foot-high chimney carried away the ash. Made of local brick, the chimney remains a prominent Mission landmark.

ONE OF THE PUMPING PLANTS
OF THE M. L. I. CO.
MISSION, TEXAS.

By 1911, the two 36-inch centrifugal pumps provided water at 75,000 gallons per minute. A planned third unit would increase pumping capacity to 115,000 gallons per minute. This postcard shows the interior of one of the Mission Land Improvement Company pump stations.

WE
PROVE IT

MISSION LAND
IMPROVEMENT CO.
INCORPORATED
MISSION, HIDALGO CO.
TEXAS

This 1911 promotional brochure described Mission's railroad facilities, businesses, schools and churches, climate, irrigation system, and the productivity of crops such as cotton, corn, onions, cabbage, grapes, beans, alfalfa, citrus, and figs. A testimonial from William Jennings Bryan, dated December 8, 1909, supported the "water contract" offered by Conway. The colors of the elaborate cover illustration are green with details in shades of dark orange and brown.

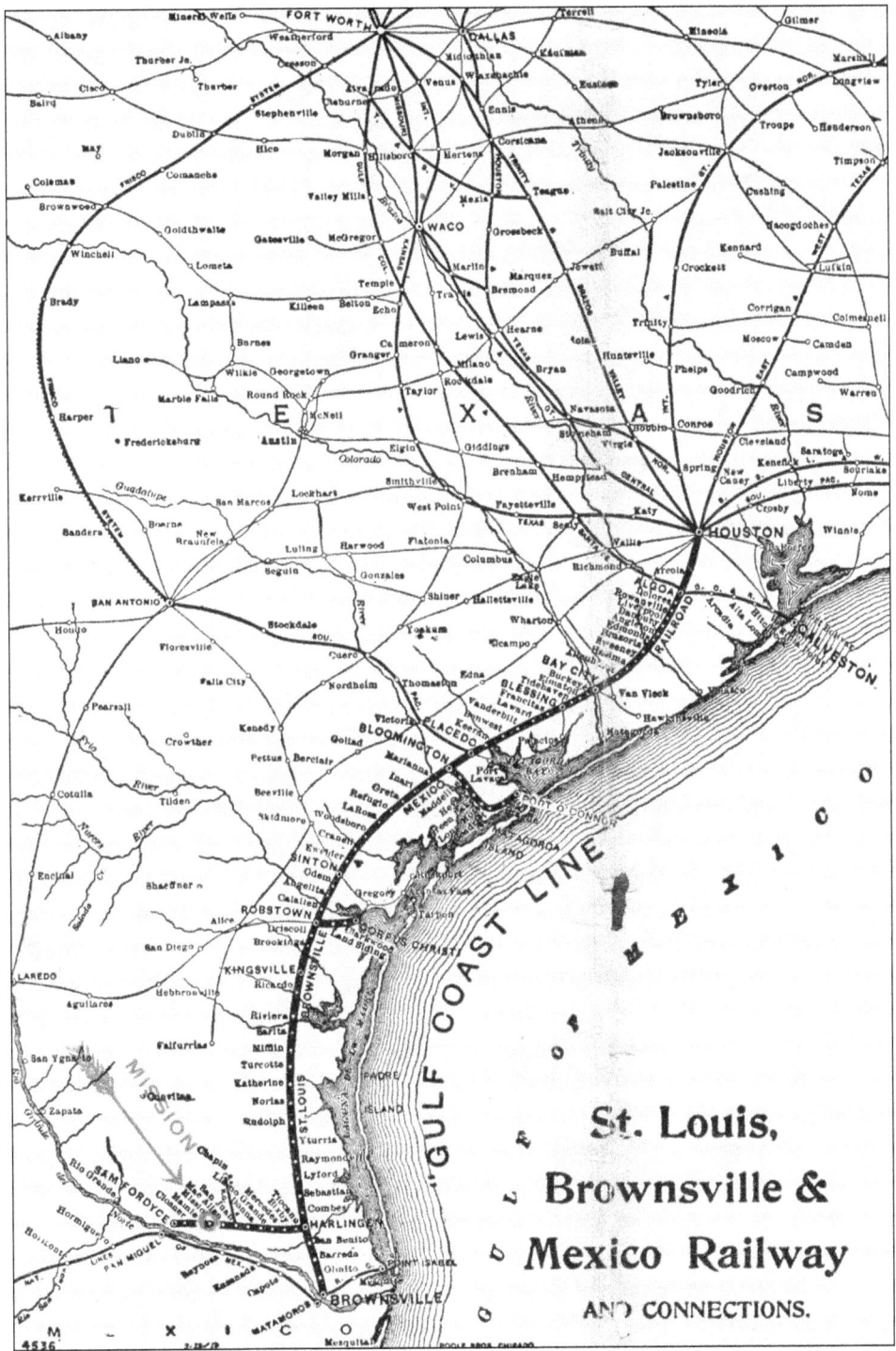

This map showing the route of the St. Louis, Brownsville, and Mexico Railway, with connections at Harlingen to the Sam Fordyce branch running east and west, appeared in the 1911 brochure. An arrow points to Mission. To sell tracts of land, shipment of produce by rail was as important as irrigation. (The town of Sam Fordyce, near Sullivan City, is gone, but Chapin is now Edinburg.)

The 1911 brochure featured bountiful crops of "early spring" potatoes. Requiring a growth season lasting only 10 weeks to three months, the Mission potatoes were ready for shipment in March.

Bermuda onions, shown here in the 1911 brochure, were an especially successful crop in Mission. In 1910, the South Texas Truck Growers' Association reported 135 acres of onions grown by 17 farms, totaling 61,985 crates for net returns of $73,560, which averaged $1.19 per crate.

The Mission Canal Company moved into this two-story brick building in 1909. In 1939, John H. Shary built an office building at this site (900 Doherty Avenue) to house his business enterprises. The Shary Building served as Mission City Hall from 1960 to 2002 and since 2002 as the Mission Historical Museum. This image shows a crowd gathering to listen to a speech given by William Jennings Bryan (center, standing).

One of the Midwesterners drawn to Mission was Nebraskan William Jennings Bryan, orator, author, and statesman, who purchased 173 acres near La Lomita Mission in 1909. After the flood of that year inundated the property, Conway offered Bryan a 200-acre tract on higher ground, which Bryan accepted. He built a winter home in Mission in 1910. Bryan (center) stands adjacent to the flag.

The first Fourth of July parade took place in 1909. Residents in wagons, buggies, and automobiles rode down Lomita Boulevard toward picnic grounds in an ebony grove on a small hill, later the site of the Cactus Tea Room, near the Roy Conway home. Sand and rain storms often ruined the parades. The 1910 parade is shown here at Lomita and Tenth Street. Note Ira J. Wright's Pure Food Grocery (right).

Dated April 1911, this picnic shared by Mission residents occurred near the Rio Grande. According to Laura Frances Murphy, arriving with her family in 1910, parents met with teachers at a picnic on the first day of school to review plans for the school year and to volunteer their help with holiday programs. Picnics, barbecues, hayrides, card parties, fiestas, and community dances at the movie theater were popular social occasions.

The Women's Tuesday Club arranged for construction of a bandstand in the park near the railroad station in 1910. Seated are members of the Women's Tuesday Club; standing behind them is the Mission Booster Band. The band provided music for all kinds of entertainment, including the Fourth of July parades, until about 1920.

Tom Humason came to Mission in 1910 to establish the Mission Booster Band. Shown here in 1911, the band members are, from left to right, the following: (first row) Tom Humason, Rudolf Rome, Oliver Swinnea, Lynn Wright, ? Parks, and C. P. Wright; (second row) Oscar Swinnea, Oliver Wakeman, Perry Wright, Robert Jeffreys (Jeffries), Harry L. Carpenter (behind Jeffries), Virgil Lott, Mel Parke, Maurice Rome, ? McPhee, Matthew Kendall, and Al Kelly.

Mission's first fraternal society, the Knights of Pythias, formed in 1910. Fraternal societies, whose meetings were attended only by men, sponsored auxiliary organizations for women. Mission's Zaragoza Lodge of the Woodmen of the World (WOW), a popular national fraternal organization, is shown here about 1918.

Mission members of the Freemasons and the Eastern Star received their charters in 1912. Many of the Knights of Pythias members joined the Masons. Officers in this undated composite are, from left to right, (top row) H. P. Peterson, L. F. Milliken, H. C. Jeffries (center), E. P. Congdon, and E. E. Scoggins; (bottom row) J. H. Marcell, A. P. Wright, and F. L. Brown.

Operation of the irrigation system proved to be more expensive than Conway planned, probably due to the 90-percent water loss through the earth-sided canals, which were not lined with concrete until many years later. Conway refused to charge more than the $1 per acre he had promised for irrigation water, causing him to operate at a loss. A national financial panic made borrowing money difficult, and the Mission Canal Company, with a debt of $225,000 secured with real estate, entered receivership on November 23, 1912. John H. Shary purchased the Conway interests in 1914. Conway continued to sell land but on a smaller scale than before. He is shown with Emma Conway in an undated photograph.

At the time of his death on February 11, 1931, the "Father of Mission" was 71. After a funeral service at St. Paul's Catholic Church, he was buried at Laurel Hill Cemetery. An obituary in the *Mission Enterprise* described him as "a straight, honest, fine gentleman, one of the squarest ever known, ever optimistic, true, clean, a lover of his home and family, and will be missed by his many friends from all over the Valley. . . . The funeral procession was one of the largest ever known here, all business houses and offices closing during the funeral hour." Today there can be no doubt that John J. Conway would be proud of his 100-year-old city.

Three

HOME SEEKERS BUILD
A COMMUNITY

During the early years, Mission businesses and residents either dug their own water wells or purchased water delivered in barrels. The water, collected from the river or the canals and poured into privately owned barrels, had to be strained and boiled for drinking and cooking. A barrel of water cost about 25¢. On July 18, 1911, voters approved Mission's first bond issue of $15,000 to build a water works.

After a lengthy courtship, Roy Conway married Dale Pickler, daughter of a U.S. Congressman from Faulkton, South Dakota, on June 12, 1915. Dale Conway (1887–1980), who came to Mission as a bride, was active in many civic organizations. Their son died in early childhood, but daughter Mary Alice (Mrs. Scott Martin) remains a Mission resident. From left to right are John Conway, Mary Alice Conway, and Roy Conway around 1924.

The Conways built a house on the north side of what is now Twentieth Street, within the present golf course. The south-facing home stood near an orchard. John Conway lived here between trips to the Midwest. Mary Alice walked to school, and her first job helping Genevieve Jeffries, caterer and owner of the Cactus Tea Room, paid 50¢ per event, a generous sum during the Great Depression.

The A. P. Wright home, built in 1909, is shown as it appeared around 1918. Wright planted one of the first citrus groves at Mission, and he experimented with state and federal government-supplied plants. In 1919, Wright received an offer of $1,750 per acre for his grove and nursery, which he turned down, but he later sold lots from the nursery. The home remains standing.

The Dawson home, in this undated photograph, stood at Tenth and Dunlap Streets, now a grocery store parking lot. Ed and Helen Dawson opened a general store on Lomita Boulevard. While Helen attended to customers, daughters Cleo and Carrie played and took naps in the store. Their home had its own water supply, indicated by the windmill, and a neat picket fence.

William Jennings Bryan (center, wearing hat and open coat) stands outside his new home, about 2 miles north of the city, around 1910. Mary Bryan left in 1911, but W. J. Bryan, with several family members, remained until 1912, when newly elected Pres. Woodrow Wilson appointed him to a cabinet position as secretary of state. In 1916, Bryan sold the house, today a private home (not open to the public).

The home of William and Eloisa Vela Doherty on Miller Avenue was a Mission showplace. Eloisa Vela, daughter of pioneer Macedonio Vela, grew up at Laguna Seca Ranch and graduated from Incarnate Word College in Brownsville. Owner of El Jardín de Flores ("garden of flowers") Ranch on the river, she provided a picnic area there, converted a stock tank to a swimming pool, and held barbecues for Mission residents.

47

By 1921, the date of this photograph, Mission neighborhoods were well established. This unusual image shows the backyard of the Walter M. Dooley residence and that of Eloisa Doherty in the distance. Dooley (1885–1948) first came to Mission from Arkansas in 1909, then brought his wife, four sons, and one daughter in 1910. A produce shipper, he served a term as county commissioner.

Residences in Oblate Addition.   MISSION, Texas.

When the Oblates of Mary Immaculate sold their *porciones* to Conway and Hoit, they reserved some land for their own use and sold residential lots to create the neighborhood shown in this undated postcard. Today the Oblate District is identified by signs. In 1916, the Oblate Fathers signed a 99-year lease with the City of Mission for a public park, now opposite St. Paul's Catholic Church.

In 1910, the Oblate Fathers built a wooden church and parish house in Mission, shown here. The dedication of Our Lady of the Mission Catholic Church, which took place on January 20, 1911, included a blessing of the new church bell, called "Eloisa," to honor Eloisa Vela Doherty. A new school with two classrooms and a stage opened in 1914 with 102 students; the teachers were two Sisters of Mercy from Laredo.

The church partially burned in 1926. After restoration, the buildings became part of the school and the convent for the Sisters of Mercy. A Mission Revival–style brick church (shown here) and a new rectory were constructed across the street in Block 105, under the direction of the Reverend Emilio LeCourtois, O.M.I. The building was dedicated and renamed Our Lady of Guadalupe Catholic Church on November 20, 1927.

Members of St. Paul's Catholic Church worshiped at La Lomita Chapel until 1913, when they built the first St. Paul's Church. Fr. Charles Siradis, O.M.I. was the first pastor. A tornado destroyed the building on May 7, 1919, and a new church (seen here) was blessed on March 7, 1920. In 1946, the church came under the jurisdiction of the Diocese of Corpus Christi. The present church and rectory were dedicated on December 7, 1960.

St. Paul's Catholic Church, without the steeple, became known as Shalom Hall (seen here) from 1960 until 1990 and served the congregation for receptions, weddings, and meetings. Although replaced by a new building in 1990, remnants of Shalom Hall remain. The round window is now installed in the church, and the front doors provide an entrance to the prayer garden.

Rev. Samuel M. Glasgow preached the first Protestant sermon in Mission on June 27, 1909. The congregation met in a pool hall on Lomita Boulevard. The First Presbyterian Church of Mission, founded on January 9, 1910, built this church that year on the corner of Twelfth and Doherty Streets on land donated by Conway and Hoit. Children climbed into the large tower to ring the bell on Sunday mornings.

Seventeen members, including Rev. J. W. and Ada Storms, organized the First Baptist Church on October 10, 1910. The congregation met at the Methodist church while erecting their church during 1911 (seen here). During the border troubles of 1915–1917, Reverend Storms left to serve in the National Guard, and Chaplain Ramsey (28th Infantry) became interim pastor for eight months. The mortgage-free church was dedicated on May 5, 1918.

Fourteen Mission Methodists held the first meeting of their congregation on Sunday, November 21, 1909, led by Rev. C. W. Godwin. Sunday school was organized in January 1910, and the first church service in their new building was held on the fourth Sunday in January 1910. Growth led to a new building in 1914. This 1934 postcard shows the present First United Methodist Church, built in 1925.

El Mesías United Methodist Church (*Iglesia Metodista El Mesías*) was established in 1912 in a building donated by the First United Methodist Church at Fifth and Francisco Streets. Rev. Leopoldo F. Castro was the first pastor (1912–1915). This brick church, built in 1933, served until 1960; the present church was built in 1962. El Mesías is known for its musical tradition, food pantry, and nursing program.

Beginning in 1909, children attended schools in Mission. George Wolfram taught Anglo children, grades one through seven, in a one-room pool hall. Hispanic children attended classes at the Catholic church, where they learned English, or at El Colegio Fronterizo, where Samuel Treviño taught entirely in Spanish. On April 19, 1910, Mission established an independent school district. The two-story brick building, shown here in 1911, served as elementary and high school.

By 1925, the school district included a new high school, a junior high school, and a primary school (later Woodrow Wilson Elementary). Hispanic children attended South Mission Elementary School (named for Theodore Roosevelt in 1927), the only fully accredited school for Spanish-speaking children in Texas. After sixth grade, they went to North Mission School (junior high) and to Mission High School, shown in this undated photograph.

This undated image shows the first home economics class offered at Mission High School. The students are, from left to right, Vina Madsen, Althea Wright, Ardis Robertson, Lucille Burgoon, Jane Hunter, Cleo Dawson, Christine Simpson, Carrie Dawson, Mamie Drummond, and Ruth Coffman. The instructor, not shown, was Mrs. Will Wood (Lulu).

Because of overcrowding due to an oil boom, the school district reorganized in 1933. Fred H. Morgan Junior High School (seen here) housed grades 8 through 11, becoming Mission High School. Enrollment continued to expand between 1930 and 1940. The high school, built between Miller and Francisco Streets around 1930, was demolished in 1985. Morgan was the first American casualty of World War I.

The champion soccer team of Hidalgo County in 1916 included numerous Mission residents. From left to right are the following: (first row) Ted Duensing, Olin Scoggins, Ray Ferguson, Ray Landry (father of Dallas Cowboys coach Tom Landry), Gouverneur Stephens, and John Spilman; (second row) Ollen Rome, Walter Melch, Walter Cronkwright, D. V. Schuchardt, Ira Dunlap, ? Norton, and Miller Armstrong.

Members of the Mission High School baseball team for the 1920–1921 season are, from left to right, Principal and Coach Ernest Poteet, Joe Bryan, Hank Evans, "Pepe" Barrera, Olwyn Dooley, Theodore Cronkwright, Lyndal Lehman, Doyt Lehman, Farrar "Cheesie" Dooley (later a business partner of Roy P. Conway), Leo Hildebrandt, unidentified, and "Frenchy" ?.

The Mission Fire Department, where Ray Landry was fire chief, held a barbecue dinner for the Mission High School athletes and cheerleaders during the 1948–1949 school year. Pictured here are Marilyn Osburn (seated, top); Norma Jean Hays (seated, at wheel); Fosteene Spikes (seated, left); Annabel Wickland (standing, center); and unidentified (standing, far right). (Courtesy Jo Ann Gibson.)

In the Mission High School class roll composite of 1923 are, from left to right and top to bottom, (first row) Leo Delbert Norman, George William Anderson, Mary Lennis Arthur, and Joseph Edmundson Bryan; (second row) Theodore Rollin Cronkwright, Helen Gertrude Bleifus, Walter Norris Dashiell, Frieda Louise Fortman, and Albert Edwin Davis; (third row) Willie Mae Kelly, Olwyn Samuel Dooley, Helen Melch, Herman Eugene Evins, and Jessie Eugene Norton; (fourth row) Cameron Lehman, Selma Alice Trapp, Ewald E. Moeller, and Ruth Irene Murphy; (fifth row) Walter Scoggins, Carroll Villere Tanner, Herschell Chester Walling, and Ruth Ruby Baker.

Henry and Fannie Ward Cauthen owned an orchard on Bryan Road. The school bus was not scheduled to stop at their house, but driver Joaquín Castro (right) knew that Wynona (center) and Jo Ann (left) were afraid of a large dog at the official stop. He paused each day to sweep out the bus, allowing the girls to get on and off at their home, seen behind the bus. Mrs. Cauthen took this photograph in 1938. (Courtesy Jo Ann Gibson.)

Four

A HAVEN
OF OPPORTUNITY

By 1912, as seen in this postcard, Mission's Hispanic business district, restricted by city charter to the south side of the railroad tracks, was growing as rapidly as its Anglo counterpart on the north side. Note the graded streets, raised sidewalks, and light poles. Citizens of Mexico, fleeing from the 1910 revolution, settled in Mission, where they found work and became permanent members of the community.

British-born Dr. Alfred Joseph Jonathan Austin (1843–1933) came to New York in 1859. After completing his medical studies, he joined the U.S. Army as a pharmacist, arriving at Fort Ringgold in Rio Grande City in 1869. In 1870, he married 16-year-old Elena Ryan. The next year, he left the army and moved to Camargo, Tamaulipas, Mexico, where he opened a medical practice. Known as *el doctor palomo* ("Doctor Dove"), he always wore white and rode a white horse to see his patients. The doctor and his large family lived in both Camargo and Mier. The family moved to Los Ebanos, Texas, in 1913 and in 1915 to Mission, where his married daughter already lived. He opened a pharmacy and medical practice in the 500 block of Lomita Boulevard. Dr. Austin donated construction materials for El Mesías Church, served as a director of the First National Bank (1923–1929), and belonged to civic and fraternal organizations. (Courtesy Elena Barrera.)

This early but undated photograph shows the general store owned by Exiquio Barrera (1883–?). The family originated in Mier, Tamaulipas, Mexico, where Capt. Santiago Barrera resided in 1780. During the 19th century, the Barrera family relocated to ranches in Brooks and Hidalgo Counties before coming to Mission. Exiquio Barrera, his wife Eutimia, and their nine children joined El Mesías, where Exiquio helped to plan and construct the first church building.

This cotton gin (seen in 1911) was one of three in Mission, along with a cottonseed oil mill. Gin machinery removed seed from fibers and baled the fibers for shipment; seed was crushed at Mission's cottonseed oil mill. In 1910, Mission farmers planted 500 acres of cotton, and in 1911, they planted 5,998 acres. Valley cotton is often the first cotton produced in the United States each year.

Baskets of beans wait on the dock for rail shipment around 1920; other crops included onions, beans, potatoes, corn, and cabbage. In 1911, farmers were also growing Egyptian wheat (a type of sorghum), broom corn, sugar cane, alfalfa, grapes, peanuts, pecans, walnuts, dates, figs, and citrus fruit (oranges, lemons, grapefruit, and kumquats).

Crates of produce were brought to Mission by the wagonload for local sale and for rail shipment all over the country. Hispanic field workers plowed with horses or mules, cultivated with hand tools, and hand-picked crops, earning from 50¢ to 75¢ per day and providing their own room and board. Horses cost about $50 per head and mules cost about $75 per head in 1911.

A Hispanic middle class developed early in Mission. Salomón Chapa (far right) stands outside his general store, La Reinera, Mercancias en General, at 409 Lomita Boulevard in 1921. Note the water barrel, brick facade, and large sign above the porch, giving the wooden building a substantial and permanent appearance.

Eighteen-year-old José María Chapa (left) and Salomón Chapa (right), store owner and father of José, stand inside La Reinera on April 14, 1921. General stores like this one provided a wide assortment of products, ranging from food and clothes to household goods such as bedding and cookware, herbal and patent medicines and liniments, and treats such as candy and bottled drinks.

Born and raised near Camargo, Tamaulipas, Mexico, Carlos G. De la Garza received a formal education with an emphasis on business methods and opened his first store in his hometown. Because of the Mexican Revolution, he came to the United States in 1913 and opened a general store on Fourth Street across from Roosevelt Elementary School. In 1915, he married Carmen Gonzales de la Viña at Edinburg, and the family lived in a small house adjacent to the store. Around 1917, he moved the store to a wooden building at 716 Lomita Boulevard (shown above). This exceptional image of the interior shows a wide range of merchandise. De la Garza (left) and an unknown assistant (right) await customers. In 1924, he built a brick store at the same location (shown below). The family lived in an apartment upstairs.

In 1925, a storm brought ice and snow to the valley. The De la Garza store (far left, above) is ringed with icicles; a Texaco gasoline pump stands beside the street light. Carlos De la Garza, standing outside the store in the undated image below, was a member of the Methodist church, a Mason, and a director of the chamber of commerce. In 1936, he separated the dry goods and grocery businesses. To expand the latter into a wholesale company, he built a warehouse on Conway Avenue, north of the railroad tracks. De la Garza maintained the dry goods and grocery businesses until the late 1960s, when the family decided to concentrate on wholesale groceries. After he retired, his son Carlos and daughters Carmen and Alicia operated the wholesale grocery business at 115 East Eighth Street until 1986.

Born at La Retama Ranch in Hidalgo County, entrepreneur J. J. Cavazos (1889–1930) was educated in Hidalgo County schools and began his professional career as a bookkeeper in Falfurrias, Texas. He owned a farm and the Mission Wholesale Grocery Company, served as vice president of the First State Bank and Trust Company of Mission as well as the Cotton Belt Gin Company in Edinburg, and was a city commissioner for four years. He was a fourth-degree Knight of Columbus and a member of the Lions Club. In 1914, Cavazos married Maria del Refugio Lozano in Falfurrias. They had two daughters, Maria Louisa and Maria del Carmen. J. J. Cavazos appears with his wife and one daughter in this undated image.

Eloisa Vela Doherty was the youngest daughter of rancher Macedonio Vela, owner of the 75,000-acre Laguna Seca ("dry lake") Ranch north of Edinburg. William S. Doherty was born at Brownsville, where Eloisa attended Incarnate Word, excelling in music and art. William, a Hidalgo County treasurer, and Eloisa owned El Jardín de Flores ("garden of flowers") Ranch, about 8,000 acres within *porciones* 51 and 52, extending from the river north to the town of Mamie. Eloisa Doherty, who created a place for Mission residents to hold picnics, often worshiped at La Lomita Chapel. She lived in Mission during the school year for her daughter Mary to attend classes and at El Jardín de Flores during the summer.

Pharmacist Pedro Barrera, youngest brother of Exiquio Barrera, was born at La Reforma ("Reformation") Ranch in northwest Hidalgo County. The Barreras farmed, raising cattle and cotton for sale. Their children attended school at the ranch and at Falfurrias or Laredo. Pedro attended El Colegio Fronterizo in Mission, where Exiquio opened his general store and brother José operated a service station (later Barrera's Supply Company). In 1920, brother Cayetano (1895–1947) became the first Mexican American to graduate from Baylor Medical School. He and his wife, Josephine, a nurse, set up his medical practice in their home at 506 Miller Avenue. After Pedro became a pharmacist, the family opened a drugstore in 1925; in 1927, Dr. Barrera built a two-story addition onto the drugstore for an office and hospital. The drugstore and hospital, Barrera-Garza Wholesale (grocery), and Barrera's Supply Company occupied the entire 500 block of South Conway Avenue. By the late 1940s, the Barreras and their extended family owned a meat market, a dry goods store, a general store, and an auto repair shop in Mission.

Five

THE BORDER TROUBLES

LOMITA BOULEVARD.
MISSION, TEXAS.

This postcard, looking north on Lomita Boulevard, shows Mission in 1913. The period between 1912 and 1920 was the most turbulent in South Texas history. Contributing factors were the Mexican Revolution of 1910, which led to raids into Texas by Mexican bandits; deployment of Texas Rangers and National Guard units to the valley; World War I; and Prohibition. These events left political, financial, and emotional scars still felt today.

By 1915, downtown Mission was crowded with automobiles, horses and buggies, shoppers, and businessmen. Sammons Hardware Company, owned by building contractor Albert Sammons, is on the far left. A lone horseman observes the traffic (far right). Several Old West–style shoot-outs took place on Lomita Boulevard in 1915.

Thomas Connelly Gill (1876–1951) came to the valley in 1903, drilling water wells for the St. Louis, Brownsville, and Mexico Railway. Gill moved to Mission in 1910, and after establishing Mission's first Ford agency in 1913, he served as a mounted customs inspector, border patrolman, and scout (1915–1920). A rancher and hotel owner, he was also elected sheriff of Hidalgo County in 1930 and 1932. Tom and Charlotte Gill had four daughters.

Ed and Helen Dawson, with daughters Cleo and Carrie, came to the valley from Webb County in 1908. A skilled mechanic, Ed Dawson set up one of the first cotton gins in Mission. He and Helen operated a general store on Lomita Boulevard. Ed died in 1920, and Carrie passed away around the same time. By 1931, Helen (right) owned her home, the store building, and a 40-acre citrus grove.

Cleo and Carrie spent much of their early childhood in the store, playing and sleeping behind the counters. After Helen's death in 1940, Cleo wrote the novel *She Came to the Valley*, published in 1943, which described their lives during the exciting days of the "border troubles" and featured Helen as the heroine of the story. The clerks and the date of this image are unidentified.

Alois Dondlinger's grocery store was built on Lomita Boulevard about where the Drummond Furniture Store had stood in 1910. Dondlinger also owned an ice cream parlor. Al Whittlesey is shown driving Dondlinger's delivery truck in 1917.

William Schafer, a native of Missouri, was living in a Mission boardinghouse when Kate Knowles, enumerator for the U.S. Census of 1910, interviewed him on May 11. He was literate and a canal construction contractor. Grocer Ira J. Wright lodged with Schafer, who owned this saloon in 1914. The men shown here are unidentified.

The Mexican Revolution of 1910 turned groups of politically inspired revolutionaries into bandits. By 1914, raiders were crossing the Rio Grande to steal livestock, rob stores, and burn farms and ranches throughout the valley before escaping to the safety of Mexico. Sheriff's deputies and Texas Rangers retaliated, often indiscriminately. Mexican refugees and Texas residents lived in constant fear. However, Mission (seen here looking north along Lomita Boulevard in 1915) continued to grow.

The "border troubles" achieved national attention, and thousands of National Guardsmen and U.S. soldiers flooded into the valley to restore order. Troops K and L of the 3rd U.S. Cavalry Regiment, led by Capt. (later Maj. Gen.) Frank R. McCoy, arrived in Mission on June 1, 1915, followed by Troop F of the 6th U.S. Cavalry Regiment on September 13, 1915. Here soldiers from Troop K, 3rd U.S. Cavalry, pause in their work.

Bakers and cooks, F troop,
6th Cav., Mission, Tex.

These bakers and cooks, from Troop F, 6th U.S. Cavalry, were photographed in their field kitchen. The baker on the far right is holding a pan of biscuits. The heat of a valley summer, and the heat of the kitchen, would have made working conditions difficult.

CAVALRY CAMP MISSION TEX.

This cavalry camp at Mission shows temporary barracks, tents, and sheds for the horses. The first pump station and chimney (far right) place the camp along the river, not far from La Lomita. Although there were no bandit raids on Mission, engagements occurred nearby at Cavazos Crossing on September 3, 4, and 5, 1915, and at Ojo de Agua on October 21, 1915.

76

Company F of the 28th Infantry (seen here), plus New York's "Fighting Second" Regiment and a motorcycle corps, swelled the population of Mission. At Thanksgiving, some 600 soldiers entertained civilian spectators with feats of horsemanship. A civilian visitor from Illinois described a picnic lunch in the shade; picking citrus fruit, figs, and bananas; and looking across the river for (unseen) bandits. Farmers were already planting onions and cabbages for the winter market.

The soldiers generally provided for themselves, indicated by this bakery, and purchased anything else they needed in Mission, boosting the city's economy. As the crisis passed, bored soldiers got into trouble, and many residents wished they would leave. A rumor that typhus had contaminated Mission's water supply caused the soldiers' redeployment to McAllen, although both cities acquired their water from the same source. The negative publicity slowed Mission's growth.

Mission, H___ of __ ___ fru__, Nov 11 1929

The presence of thousands of professional U.S. Army and federalized National Guard troops in the valley stopped the bandit raids and brought the "border troubles" to a peaceful end. To benefit from their quiet duty on the border, the troops conducted frequent cavalry and artillery exercises along and north of the Rio Grande, which provided crucial training. In 1917, the soldiers and Red Cross nurses at the field hospitals returned to their home states or military bases, but later that year, most were sent to Europe to serve in World War I. Roy P. Conway enlisted in the army in 1918, served stateside at Camp Lee, Virginia, and was discharged as a first lieutenant in January 1919. After establishing an insurance agency, Conway served as chairman of Selective Service Board No. 2 in 1940 and joined the Texas Defense Guard in 1942, remaining in the reserves until 1956, when he retired as a lieutenant colonel. A strong tradition of military service characterizes Mission today. Here residents watch a parade along Lomita Boulevard on Veterans Day, November 11, 1929.

Six

THE LEGACY OF
JOHN H. SHARY

To provide irrigation for development of farmland, Conway and Hoit built three lift stations between 1908 and 1910. John H. Shary bought the assets of the Mission Canal Company in 1914 and established the United Irrigation Company in 1915. Shary extended the canals, improved the lift stations, and installed concrete pipes for water distribution. Irrigation pipes are now underground, but concrete standpipes containing valves remain distinctly characteristic of the valley.

Born in Denmark in 1873, George Hansen came to the United States with his parents at the age of 15, settling in Minneapolis. George and Tena married in the late 1890s (shown here), and they owned a dairy farm. George's brother-in-law worked for Shary, and after making an excursion trip sponsored by Shary, the Hansens moved to Mission. George worked as a farmer, painter, carpenter, rock mason, and bricklayer.

George and Tena Hansen had a family of six children. Shown here moving a shed at their property on North Stewart Road are, from left to right, George and sons Harry, Rich, and Milton. The mules were called Jenny and Jack.

John H. Shary (1872–1945) was the youngest of five children born to Robert and Rose Sary (pronounced and Americanized to "Shary"), who had left Prague, Bohemia (now the Czech Republic), to settle in Nebraska. During high school, John Shary worked at a drugstore, earning $1.50 per week. At the age of 18, he became one of the youngest registered pharmacists in Nebraska. After attending college for two years, he and a partner opened a drugstore. Although the drugstore earned a profit, Shary went to work as a salesman for a California redwood lumber company. He traveled widely and began to recognize his future as a land developer. After buying ranchland near San Antonio and selling it for a profit, he formed the International Land and Investment Company of Omaha in 1904. Between 1904 and 1911, Shary and his partner, George H. Paul, bought and sold about 268,000 acres for cotton production in the Corpus Christi area. By 1912, with most of their holdings gone, Paul left for Colorado, and Shary came to Mission.

On November 13, 1922, John Shary married Mary E. O'Brien at Carthage, Missouri. A keenly intelligent businesswoman, she had worked for Shary at his International Land and Investment Company in Omaha, and she remained active and influential in his Mission business and social interests. Shary was a 32nd-degree Mason and a member of the Elks and Woodsmen fraternal organizations. John and Mary had no children, but Mary's niece, Marialice Roetelle, joined them when she was 15, and they formally adopted her when she was 21. Marialice took the Shary name even before her adoption and remained very close to the couple. Marialice married future Texas governor Allan Shivers at the Shary home in 1937. After John Shary's death on November 6, 1945, Mary O'Brien Shary continued to live at their estate in Sharyland, a subdivision of Mission, until her death in 1959. Both are buried in a beautiful mausoleum near the Shary home. (The date and location of this image are unknown.)

4063   SHARY LAKE COUNTRY CLUB, MISSION, TEXAS

In 1914, John Shary began building a home, seen in this postcard, on Shary Boulevard. Completed in 1917, it also served as a clubhouse for prospective land buyers for several years. The house overlooked a 3-acre lake, and a bathhouse stood at one end of the lake. The Shary family hosted dignitaries and held social events at their elegant home. The property now belongs to the University of Texas–Pan American.

Shary, who enjoyed fishing and playing cards, built this yacht club at Port Isabel as a resort. Among his friends were Vice Pres. John Nance Garner, journalist Ernie Pyle, oilman Jesse H. Jones, Texas governor Coke R. Stevenson, Mission developer Lloyd M. Bentsen, and author Dale Carnegie. Never reluctant to cross social boundaries, Shary worked closely with his Anglo and Hispanic employees, knew their families, and helped them if needed.

Edward Oppenheimer, owner of the Valley Mercantile Company, was born and educated in San Francisco. In 1912, he married Goldye Lazarus of Louisville, Kentucky, and they came to Mission in 1913. Oppenheimer was active in the Masonic Lodge, Mystic Shrine, and Mission Rotary Club. A friend of John Shary, Oppenheimer is credited with the early promotional slogan "Mission: Home of the Grapefruit" in 1921.

Seen here about 1931, Shary bought 16,000 acres at Mission in 1913 and, by 1922, increased his holdings to over 49,000 acres, known as Sharyland. His first commercial crop of grapefruit, planted in 1915 and harvested in 1922, was cleaned and graded by hand. In 1923, after a trip to research the citrus industry in California, he built the first commercial citrus-packing plant in Mission and formed the Texas Citrus Fruit Growers Exchange.

This aerial view, dated 1925, shows northbound Shary Road. The Texas Citrus Fruit Growers Exchange office and packing shed stand near the railroad tracks at U.S. Business Highway 83. The large building north of the office is Sharyland School. Shary set up the Sharyland Independent School District in 1921, oversaw construction of the high school in 1924, and served as school board president from 1921 until 1939.

These women, seen during the late 1920s, are fruit packers at the Texas Citrus Fruit Growers Exchange packing shed. Second from the right is Mildred Hansen, who later married Gene Autry Chesshire, the supervisor. Workers sorted, cleaned, graded, and packed citrus fruit for shipping in wooden crates. By 1945, there were more than 6 million citrus trees in Hidalgo County and about 2 million in Mission.

In December 1930, at
the height of the citrus
season, John and Mary
Shary held a party at
their mansion to promote
citrus products. Shown
here are (left) "King"
John Shary and (right)
"Queen" Emogene Baker,
wife of Hidalgo County
Sheriff A. Y. Baker. The
party inspired dreams
for an even larger event.
Paul Ord, chairman
of the Young Men's
Business League (an
organization affiliated
with the Mission
Chamber of Commerce),
began to make plans
for a pageant, a parade,
and a coronation ball.
Additional activities,
all held on one day,
included a football game,
fruit-packing contests,
and a flying circus.
The festival, designed
to establish Mission as
the hub of the valley's
citrus industry, proved
remarkably successful.
The Texas Citrus Fiesta
has been held every
year since 1932, except
for 1933 due to a severe
hurricane and the years
during World War II.

In 1930, Shary created the Shary Products Company to find an economical use for grapefruit of less than the highest grades. The company soon began commercial bottling of grapefruit juice, calling their product Rio Rey ("river king"). This image shows the interior of the Shary Products Company bottling plant as it appeared on February 11, 1931.

The Texas Fruit Growers Exchange, an organization dedicated to the efficient and profitable marketing and distribution of citrus products, evolved into today's Texas Citrus Exchange. This arrangement of Rio Rey grapefruit juice, advertised as "pure unadulterated juice," was presented at an early Texas Citrus Fiesta. Because of his innovative and far-reaching contributions, John H. Shary is known as the "Father of the Texas Citrus Industry."

Shown here is "Queen Citriana I," who was Marguerite Daniel (later Mrs. Winston Jenkins). Produce shipper W. D. Toland was "King Grapefruit." Popular radio personality Moulton "Ty" Cobb of Weslaco served as master of ceremonies. Women representing valley cities and organizations participated in the pageant. Tickets to the Queen's Ball cost $1.65 per couple, and the ball took place at the Sprowl Fruit Packing Plant in Mission—the only building large enough for everyone.

Queen's Float

First Annual Texas Citrus Fiesta
Dec 4, 1932. Mission Photo by Gardner

The queen's float (seen here) was one of 27 in the 1932 Texas Citrus Fiesta parade. In 1934, the Parade of Oranges boasted 34 floats, and new activities included a children's parade and a golf tournament. By 1935, parade costumes were being made from fruits and vegetables, leaves, seeds, and flowers glued to a cloth foundation. Judges presented awards for the best floats and product costumes.

Program

TEXAS CITRUS FIESTA

Inaugurating

Citrus Week in Texas

MISSION

"Home of the Grapefruit"

ACCOMMODATION HEADQUARTERS
Caldwell Building
CITRUS JUICES SERVED ALL DAY

The Texas Citrus Fiesta program (cover shown here) for December 6–8, 1935, lists the festivities as follows: on Friday night was the coronation of Queen Citriana III and a ball for the queen and her court; on Saturday were concerts, fruit packing and box making competitions, a formal dedication of the Mission Municipal Airport, a Boy Scout demonstration, a product costume show, and another ball; and on Sunday was a golf tournament.

Shown here during a January 1948 parade in the Hi-Y Club car (sponsored by the junior high school coach) are, from left to right, the following: (seated in front) Robert Rome, Ted Jones, and Dick Volz (owner and driver of the car); (seated on top) unidentified, Bill Dondlinger, Jack Landry, Billy Gray, Robert Volz, Jack Peterson, and Dick Brown. (Courtesy Jo Ann Gibson.)

During the 1930s, the product costumes were featured at public events throughout Texas. In 1938, the Texas Citrus Fiesta was rescheduled from December to January. Fox Movietone News presented valley bathing beauties in a pool full of grapefruit. *National Geographic* published a color section on the valley and product costumes in 1939. The fiesta resumed after a hiatus during World War II. Shown here is the *c.* 1947 queen's float.

Hayes-Sammons Hardware Company sponsored this Mission High School Future Farmers of America float in 1948. June Cluster (center) was the Future Farmers of America sweetheart. Floats provided by churches, civic and social organizations, and businesses were designed and built by volunteers, who spent hundreds of hours planning the queen's ball, constructing the floats, and creating the product costumes.

This historical marker, issued by the Texas State Historical Commission in 1964, stands at the entrance gate to the Shary mansion. Besides land development, irrigation, and citrus, Shary's interests included education, banking, newspaper publishing, and investment companies. He served as chairman of the committee that promoted extension of the Intracoastal Waterway from Corpus Christi to Brownsville. John H. Shary's legacy lives on in many Mission place names and enterprises.

Maurine Duncan Nickolaus, who came to Mission in 1935 to teach school, designed and made many product costumes throughout the years. In 1947, for example, she designed 22 gowns for the pageant, which was held at Moore Field. The Maurine Duncan Award is given to those who contribute many years of talent and support to the pageant. Begun in 1932, the Texas Citrus Fiesta remains a popular cultural event. Many of the fiesta gowns are on exhibit at the Mission Historical Museum. Shown here is Wilma Cutler, Queen Citriana for 1950.

Seven

RAPID GROWTH OF THE YOUNG CITY

By 1920, over 3,800 citizens lived in Mission. Roque Alaniz provided taxi service with his fleet of eight Fords carrying workers to oil fields and elected officials to Austin. Texas Highway Number 4 (U.S. Business Highway 83), paved between Pharr and Mamie in 1924, reached the Starr County line in 1926. Door-to-door mail delivery began in 1925. Lomita Boulevard, seen here in 1931, shows a substantial business district.

In 1903, Charles J. Volz, born and educated in Indiana, settled with his parents and siblings in Brownsville, where they farmed rice and celery. He married Rose K. Meyer of Cincinnati, Ohio, in 1904, and they returned to Brownsville. Around 1906, he bought land south of the Mission townsite, built a house, and grew vegetable crops. In 1908, Volz bought citrus trees from Florida and planted an orchard. (John J. Conway later established his own orchard across the road.) Volz experimented with different varieties of grapefruit, sold nursery stock, and participated in marketing activities. His orchard became a showplace for excursion train visitors. His wife, Rose—who is credited with suggesting the name "Mission" for the new city—allowed visitors to pick grapefruit but charged them 25¢ for each one. By 1931, Volz owned 65 acres of citrus trees (mostly grapefruit) on his 80-acre farm. He was active in St. Paul's Catholic Church and served on the board of the Mission Independent School District. The parents of four children, Charles and Rose Volz are shown here about 1931.

Guenther Weiske came to Mission in 1911. A German native, he had a formal education in agriculture and a wealth of technical training. He bought land along the river for farming but began to make bricks from the yellow clay soil. In 1912, he supplied bricks for construction of St. Peter's Novitiate. Weiske formed the Mission Brick Company in 1923. This envelope displays La Lomita Chapel as a prominent symbol.

In 1923, Weiske and a partner purchased machinery for extruding bricks. During the 1930s, he replaced wood fires with gas ovens to dry the brick, and in 1940, Weiske and a new partner bought additional drying machinery. Known as Valley Brick and Tile Company, the factory made drainage tile, canal lining brick, face brick, and other products. Two workers show the company's motto on the door of their delivery truck.

Organized on July 1, 1909, by Conway and six partners, the First State Bank of Mission opened on August 4, 1909, with $12,500 in capital stock and total resources of $15,532. Located first at 900 Doherty Avenue, in 1911 the bank moved to a new two-story building on Lomita Boulevard, shown here in the winter of 1925–1926. Under John H. Shary as president (1922–1944), the bank began to offer trust services and changed its name to First State Bank and Trust Company in 1927.

The Gulf Refining Company opened in 1920. By the 1930s, the distributorship (seen here) served 10 retail outlets in Mission and the surrounding area. The business was located at the corner of Ninth Street and Oblate Avenue. Pictured here are, from left to right, Lee Roy Friedrichs; Calvin Friedrichs; (attendants) ? Menke, unidentified, and Ed Danks; and L. T. Friedrichs. Calvin Friedrichs, a gunner's mate in the U.S. Navy, served in the Philippines during World War II.

By 1925, Mission had built a handsome brick city hall, seen in this undated postcard view, and immediately behind it stands the fire department. A 1925 promotional brochure states that Mission maintained the following: a population of almost 6,000; "a well organized fire department, equipped with modern fire fighting machines;" 3 miles of paved streets with more being planned; concrete sidewalks; an "up-to-date" sewer system; and bonds approved for the "installation of a modern water works system." Mission also had "four wholesale houses," three hotels, two railroads, and two movie theaters. Organizations included a "live commercial Club, composed of wide-awake business men," a civic league, Rotary Club, Oddfellows, Rebekahs, and Freemasons as well as a Parent-Teacher Association. The city boasted almost 800 houses within the city limits as well as nine churches, a public school district with a territory of 22 square miles, and a tax rate of 75¢ per $100 of property value.

The Mission Volunteer Fire Department was organized around 1916, when the city spent $150 for a chemical cart and appointed Tom Humason as fire chief. On April 1, 1930, Mayor G. F. Dohrn (1926–1930) appointed Harold Ray Landry (left) as fire chief. With the exception of 1959–1961, Landry served as fire chief until he retired on December 1, 1972. Born in Illinois in 1898, Ray was the son of Fred and Lillian Landry and one of six children. As a result of the loss of two of the children and the chronic illness of Ray and his sister Viola, the Landry family moved to the warmer climate of Mission in February 1912. Fred Landry bought land and began farming. However, his skills as a master brick mason kept him so busy that the family moved into town, where he could be closer to his projects. Ray graduated from Mission High School in 1918 and attended Texas A&M University. He married Ruth Coffman in 1920, and they had four children. Thomas Wade Landry, their third child, became the fabled coach of the Dallas Cowboys football team.

On December 7, 1935, during the annual Texas Citrus Fiesta, residents celebrated the opening of the Mission Municipal Airport at what is now Mission High School. The U.S. Postal Service issued special covers (specially stamped envelopes) for the occasion. A bag with postal envelopes lies on the ground (center). Lieutenant Colonel Richards spoke at the formal dedication of the airport. Although the individuals here are unidentified, the occasion of the photograph is confirmed from other sources.

In 1932, after assessing the cost in time and fees to play golf in other valley cities since Mission did not have a course, Roy P. Conway and friends Roy Buckley and E. P. Congdon presented their concept for a five-hole course to John H. Shary, who owned the land where they wanted to build. Shary agreed to lease the land to the city for 25 years and expanded the area to accommodate nine holes. The Shary Municipal Golf Course was built during the spring of 1933. In December, the first Golden Grapefruit Tournament took place during the Texas Citrus Fiesta, becoming an annual event. After John Shary's death, his daughter, Marialice Shary Shivers, donated the land to the city. In 1992, the Mission City Council approved a plan to add a driving range and bought a portion of the original Roy Conway home site from Scott and Mary Alice (Conway) Martin. Shown in this undated photograph are (center) W. R. Parrish and (second from right) J. C. "Red" Hall, who was the golf professional at the Shary Municipal Golf Course; the other men are unidentified.

Elisa Emma Rico Alvarez (1920–2003) was born in Mexico City and moved to Texas in 1925. The Rico family lived in Mission, where Elisa attended high school. She worked for the Department of Immigration and Naturalization and the Selective Services Local Board. When she joined the U.S. Navy in October 1941, she was recognized as the first valley woman to enlist in the armed forces in World War II. Assigned to duty at Pearl Harbor, Hawaii, as a yeoman second class, she served in the U.S. Navy from 1941 until the war ended in 1945. She returned to the valley upon receiving an honorable discharge. In 1949, she married José Carlos Alvarez of Brownsville, and they raised their six children in the Houston area. Elisa Alvarez worked for the Social Security Administration, retiring in 1977. After obtaining her bachelor's and master's degrees in bilingual education, she taught fourth graders in Houston for 10 years and retired once again in 1991. She then returned to college to further her painting skills, as art was a passion she pursued throughout her life.

Elisa Emma Rico Alvarez
U.S. Navy
1941–1945

Following in the footsteps of Mission women like Olympia Olivarez Peña, a U.S. Navy nurse (1942–1945), and Anne Belle Forquer Siegel Adams, U.S. Navy (1942–1945), Mary Capotosta Van Deventer also joined the U.S. Navy. Born in 1922 near Boston, Massachusetts, she joined WAVES, formed in July 1942, and served in the 1st Battalion, organized in March 1943. She achieved the rating of chief storekeeper in dispersing, supervising 25 men and women in the payroll department at Norfolk, Virginia. After the war, she worked for the U.S. Navy in Washington, D.C., and attended the Berlitz School of Languages. She met Al Graham of Mission, who was attending Georgetown Law School. After he graduated, they moved to Mission and had three daughters.

First Lt. Joaquin Castro (1916–1943) was born and raised in Mission. He attended Mission schools and Edinburg Junior College. He was the first Mission native to be commissioned a pilot in the U.S. Army Air Forces in the buildup to World War II, receiving his wings at Luke Field, Arizona, in November 1941. He was stationed at Hickam Field in Hawaii during the attack on Pearl Harbor on December 7, 1941. Lieutenant Castro remained in the Pacific theater, where he earned the National Defense Medal, Distinguished Flying Cross, and Air Medal with Oak Leaf Cluster. He was lost in the South Pacific on February 1, 1943.

Carlos Benjamin De la Garza, born in 1922, joined the U.S. Navy on December 9, 1942. The son of store owner Carlos G. De la Garza, he attended officer's training school at Tulane University and midshipman's school at Harvard University. This image shows De la Garza upon his graduation from Harvard in 1944. During World War II, he served on the destroyer USS *Upshur* (DD-144), which escorted carriers from Boston to Miami and across the Atlantic. When the war ended, he transferred to the aircraft carrier USS *Manila Bay*, stationed in the Pacific. Discharged on March 4, 1946, with the rank of lieutenant junior grade, De la Garza returned to Mission and worked in his father's store and wholesale grocery business. During his long career, he became a commissioner of the Hidalgo County housing authority, a director of the First National Bank of Mission, a board director of the Mission Independent School District, and a board member of El Mesías United Methodist Church. He married Angelica Gonzalez on November 17, 1944, and they had six children.

Although they shared the same last name, and Eligio "Kika" De la Garza called Carlos De la Garza "uncle," the two men were unrelated. Born in Mercedes in 1927, Kika De la Garza grew up in Mission, attending Our Lady of Guadalupe Catholic School and Mission High School. At age 17, he enlisted in the U.S. Navy. Returning home in 1946, he completed his high school education and attended Edinburg Junior College and St. Mary's University in San Antonio, where he was a member of the ROTC. During the Korean War (1950–1952), he served as a second lieutenant in the 37th Division Artillery (seen here). In 1952, he earned his law degree from St. Mary's University. The same year, while still in the army, he was elected to the Texas House of Representatives and served for six consecutive terms (1953–1965). His legislation created the Texas Water Commission, linked Edinburg Junior College with the University of Texas system, set up a statewide program of English instruction for children of preschool age, and authorized border cities and counties to build international bridges.

Eligio "Kika" De la Garza married Lucille Alamía of Edinburg on May 29, 1953, shown here at their wedding. From 1965 until 1997, he represented Texas's 15th Congressional District in the U.S. House of Representatives. A member of the Agriculture Committee beginning in 1965, he became chairman of the committee in 1981—the first Hispanic American to head a standing committee of Congress since 1917. He continued in that role for 13 years. To help the valley, his bills have sponsored improvements in the following: water and sewer systems for *colonias*; health care and housing for the elderly, veterans, and low-income citizens; the development of alternative crops and crop varieties, affordable credit, and nutrition programs; the North American Free Trade Agreement; and the construction of dams. De la Garza has received hundreds of awards and both national and international honors. The De la Garzas have three children, Jorge, Michael, and Angela.

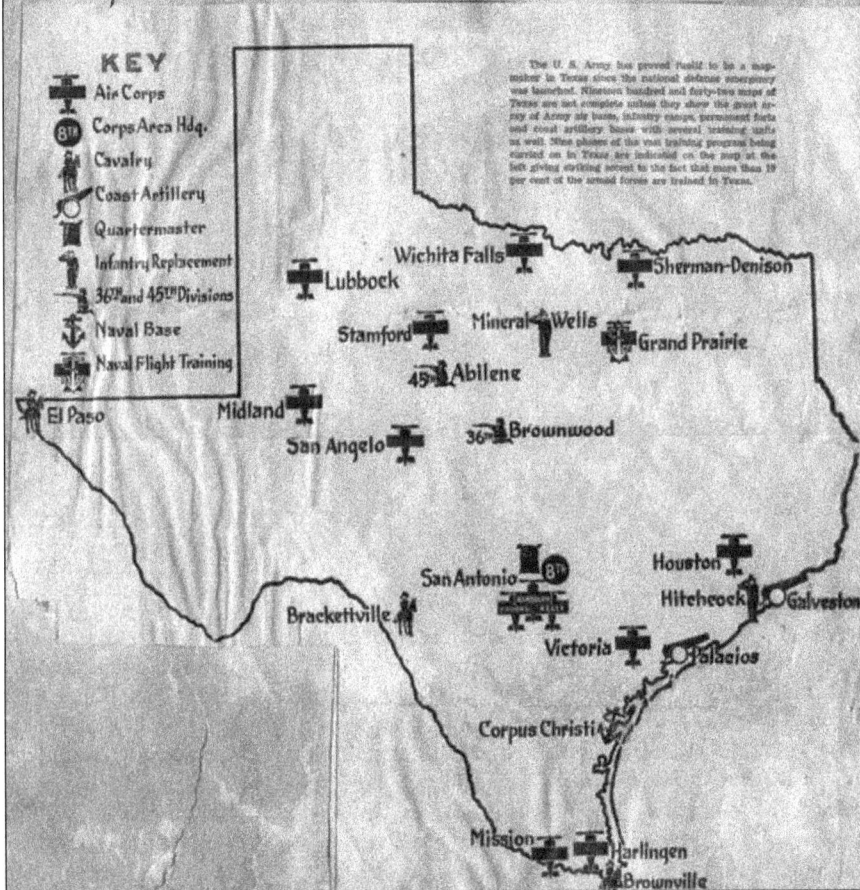

Welcome

To The Officers And Men Of

Moore Field

KEY

✈ Air Corps
🛡 Corps Area Hdq.
🐎 Cavalry
Coast Artillery
Quartermaster
Infantry Replacement
36ᵀᴴ and 45ᵀᴴ Divisions
⚓ Naval Base
Naval Flight Training

The U. S. Army has proved itself to be a mapmaster in Texas since the national defense emergency was launched. Nineteen hundred and forty-two maps of Texas are not complete unless they show the great array of Army air bases, infantry camps, permanent forts and coast artillery bases with several training units as well. Nine phases of the vast training program being carried on in Texas are indicated on the map at the left giving striking accent to the fact that more than 19 per cent of the armed forces are trained in Texas.

Wichita Falls • Sherman-Denison
Lubbock
Stamford • Mineral Wells • Grand Prairie
45 Abilene
El Paso • Midland
San Angelo • 36 Brownwood
San Antonio 8ᵀᴴ • Houston
Brackettville • Hitchcock • Galveston
Victoria • Palacios
Corpus Christi
Mission • Harlingen • Brownsville

This 1942 map of military bases in Texas shows Moore Field, about 12 miles northwest of Mission. After an initial inspection by U.S. Army representatives in 1941, officials from Mission, Edinburg, and McAllen formed an Airport Committee to create a fund to buy 1,158 acres. To speed up the process, John H. Shary and R. N. Smith bought 1,000 acres. The three cities provided $30,000, and local citizens provided the remainder to complete the land purchase. The site was then leased to the government. The land cost $7.50 per acre to buy and $10.00 per acre more to clear. In July 1941, Sen. Tom Connally announced an allotment of $4 million to build the base. Construction of runways, hangars, streets, offices, and barracks, plus a road from Mission to Moore Field, required about 1,400 people. Moore Field was named for Lt. Frank Murchison Moore, a Houston native and pilot who was killed during a combat mission over France on September 4, 1918. Moore Field opened on November 22, 1941.

The first training aircraft (AT-6) arrived in late January 1942, followed by the first class of cadets a month later. Fighter pilots, like the group shown here around 1944, completed a training class every four and a half weeks. They mastered skills in maneuvering, gunnery, radio communication, and navigation. Enlisted men who worked as mechanics kept up with physical training, drill, and weapons instruction. Women worked as mechanics, and some flew the airplanes, but they did not participate in combat exercises. About 250 civilians worked at Moore Field. The last class graduated in April 1945, and the base remained a flying school until it closed on October 31, 1945. The Tri-Cities Commercial Airport and the Weaver H. Baker Tuberculosis Hospital shared the facilities until 1954. Reactivated that year as Moore Air Force Base, some 4,000 air force pilots received military, academic, and flight training (on T-28 and T-34 propeller craft and T-37 jets) during six-month classes until December 1960. The land was deeded to the U.S. government in 1954, and since 1960, it has housed research offices of the U.S. Department of Agriculture.

The Mission Post Office, shown here soon after its construction in 1940, remained in service at this location until 1984. The school district (1984–1988) and the Mission Police Department (1989–2000) also used the building. In March 2002, the City of Mission leased it to the Mission Historical Museum for events and exhibits. The original (1942) oil-on-canvas mural by Xavier González entitled *West Texas Landscape* is on view.

The Shary Office Building, constructed in 1939 to house eight of John Shary's businesses, was designed by San Antonio architect Harvey P. Smith. A mix of Spanish Colonial Revival and Mexican Colonial styles, the two-story brick building became Mission City Hall from 1960 to 2002. Since 2002, it has been home to the Mission Historical Museum. This 1947 image shows the building decorated for the Texas Citrus Fiesta.

Businesses on Conway Avenue around 1951 included Lack's Auto Supply and Furniture Store and the Manhattan Café on the right as well as the Valley Sandwich Shop, Border Theater, Florsheim Shoe Store, and Anthony's Department Store on the left. The Border, owned by Robert N. and Dell Smith, was one of six theaters the couple built in the valley. William J. Moore, a Dallas architect, designed the building in Art Pueblo style. The air-conditioned theater featured a seating capacity of 740 (today, after renovations, there are about 500 seats). The Border opened on April 3, 1942, with *Heart of the Rio Grande*, starring Roy Rogers. Juan Barbera, a bricklayer and native of Spain, built an earlier theater called La Paz at 516 Doherty Avenue in 1912. He brought films, lecturers, actors, and musicians to Teatro La Paz. Enrique Flores Sr. bought the building in 1945 and renamed it the Rio Theater. His son, Enrique Flores Jr., converted it to an art studio and gallery called the Xochil Theater and established a nonprofit organization in 1976. Now closed, the Xochil Theater sponsored many art exhibitions, film festivals, and cultural events.

Eight

MISSION'S NOTABLE
SONS AND DAUGHTERS

Patricio Pérez of Havana, Texas, west of Mission, set a precedent for military service. A 32-year-old vaquero, Pérez volunteered for service in the U.S. (Union) Army on December 10, 1863. He enlisted as a private in the 2nd Regiment of Texas Cavalry. Commanded by Col. John L. Haynes of Rio Grande City, the 2nd Regiment engaged in campaigns in Texas, Louisiana, and Mississippi. Promoted to first sergeant in 1864, Pérez received his discharge in San Antonio on October 28, 1865.

Visiting on the porch of the Boulevard Hotel and Café (1910–1911) are, from left to right, Red Stevens, Claude Franklin, O. C. Kelly, Frank Dew, John Paul Burton, William Jennings Bryan, Charles Butterfield, and H. Peterson. Henry ? leans on the automobile. Monroe Dunlap (1857–1939) owned a general store, a lumberyard, and a citrus farm. His wife, Sarah, managed the hotel and café. Dunlap Avenue honors these pioneers.

Maurine (Yarborough) Duncan Nickolaus (1915–2009) of Shiner, Texas, came to Mission in 1935 to teach fine arts. She married Thomas Logan Duncan Jr. in 1939, and the couple had two daughters. She was the first woman on the Mission City Council (1977–1983), participated in many civic events, wrote a newspaper column, and set up the Mission Historical Society in 1972. After Logan Duncan's death (1979), she married William Nickolaus (1989). Maurine received many honors for her important contributions to Mission.

Seen here around 1940, Cleo Dawson (1902–1991) and her sister, Carrie, played in their parents' general store and attended Mission schools. In 1922, Cleo earned a bachelor's degree from Southern Methodist University in Dallas and returned to the valley to teach Spanish at Mission High School. Four years later, Cleo married George Edwin Smith, and the couple moved to Lexington, Kentucky. In 1947, she received a doctorate in psychology from the University of Kentucky. Renowned as a public speaker, she also appeared as staff psychologist on *The Merv Griffin Show* on television. Her novel *She Came to the Valley*, published in 1943, was filmed as a movie by the same title in 1977 and premiered in McAllen in 1978. Scenes shot in Mission featured residents as actors and extras. Mission honored Dr. Cleo Dawson as "The First Lady of Mission" in 1979.

Leonardo Alaniz (1899–1978), or "Leo Najo," was the first Mexican American to play professional baseball in the United States. Born in Mexico, he moved to Mission with his mother when he was nine years old. In 1918, he joined a semi-professional baseball team in Mission called the "30-30s," after the Winchester rifle. A center fielder and home run hitter, Alaniz starred in the Texas and Western Leagues between 1924 and 1932. Due to his speed as a base runner, fans called him a *conejo*, or rabbit (mispronounced *najo*). The Chicago White Sox drafted him from the San Antonio Bears in 1926. During a temporary return to the Bears, he suffered a broken leg in the outfield. His career in the major leagues ended, but he continued in the minors throughout the 1930s. Tired of the travel, he returned to Mission, where he and his wife, Elida (Garza), raised a large family and he coached baseball. The Mission High School baseball field is named in his honor. Above are Alaniz (front row, third from left) and the Southern Select team in Harlingen in 1938. (Courtesy Rene Torres.)

Thomas Wade Landry (1924–2000) was born and raised in Mission, where his father Ray Landry was a mechanic and fire chief. As quarterback, Landry led the Mission Eagles to two championships and attended the University of Texas on a football scholarship (1942). In 1943, he joined the Army Air Corps and received flight training as a B-17 bomber pilot (seen here). Stationed in England, he flew 30 combat missions over Europe. Discharged as a first lieutenant in 1945, he returned to the University of Texas, where he played fullback for the Texas Longhorns. He married Alicia Wiggs in 1949; they were the parents of a son and two daughters. After graduation (1949), he signed with the New York Yankees (New York Giants after 1950). He played until 1955 and stayed on with the Giants as an assistant defensive coach until 1959. He became head coach of the Dallas Cowboys in 1960, winning two Super Bowl championships, but left in 1989 when club owner Jerry Jones decided to replace him. Landry spent his later years managing his non-profit organization.

Eudocio "Bocho" Garcia (1926–2009) was born in Mission. He served in the U.S. Army in Japan and Korea and received an honorable discharge in 1946. As a resident of Roma for many years, he served as president of the school board, charter member of the Veterans of Foreign Wars chapter, member of the Kiwanis Club, Boy Scout leader, and city manager. During his long career, he held positions as city manager of Hidalgo and Alamo and as mayor of Bishop, near Corpus Christi. He eventually retired to Hidalgo. He and his wife, Amalia (Garcia), were the parents of one son and four daughters.

Better known as the wrestler "Tito Santana" or "El Matador," Merced Solís (born in 1953) was the son of migrant workers. He graduated from Mission High School, where he excelled in sports, and from West Texas State University, then played professional football for the Kansas City Chiefs and the British Columbia Lions. He began wrestling in 1977, winning championships in 1978, 1983–1985, and 1995. He is now a middle school teacher and coach in Roxbury, New Jersey. He and wife Leah (seen here) have three sons.

Attorney Robert Allan Shivers (1907–1985) of Lufkin married Marialice Shary at the Shary mansion in 1937. Texans elected him state senator (1935–1946), lieutenant governor (1947–1949), and governor (1949–1957). This image shows the family on July 16, 1949, during his campaign for governor. In the foreground are honor guards from Woodville (names unknown). Behind them are, from left to right, Robert Allan Jr. (born 1946), John (born 1940), and Marialice Sue (born 1947). (A third son, Brian, was born in 1952.) In the back row are, from left to right, Mary Shary, Marialice Shary Shivers, Lt. Gov. Allan Shivers, and his mother, Mrs. Robert A. Shivers (Sue).

Lloyd M. Bentsen Jr. (1921–2006), son of a valley land developer, was born and raised in Mission, graduating from Sharyland High School in 1937. An attorney, he served in the U.S. Army during World War II, earning the rank of major as a B-24 pilot and squadron commander. After the war, he returned to the valley, where he was elected Hidalgo County judge (1947) and representative from the 15th U.S. Congressional District (1949–1955). After a successful business career in Houston, he won a seat in the U.S. Senate (1971–1993). Pres. Bill Clinton appointed Bentsen secretary of the treasury (1993–1994). Bentsen and wife Beryl Ann "B.A." (Longino) had three children. Land donated by the Bentsen family in 1944 became Bentsen State Park in Mission, and in 2004, it became the headquarters of the valley's World Birding Center.

Although his family was from Mexico, Salomón S. "Sol" Marroquín was born in San Antonio in 1931. After settling in Mission in 1939, his father was the first Hispanic to own a barbershop north of the railroad tracks, which was the first air-conditioned barbershop and the only shop with a shower for clients to use. Sol Marroquín spent four years in Special Services with the U.S. Air Force in Korea and another 18 years in the Air Force Reserves, earning the rank of master sergeant. He was a city secretary for Mission, an administrator at the Mission Municipal Hospital, and a staff member for Congressman E. "Kika" De la Garza for 21 years. In the tradition of Ken Maynard of Mission, who became Hollywood's first singing cowboy, Marroquín acted in seven Hollywood films. He is the author of *Part of the Team*, a biography of Medal of Honor recipient U.S. Marine Sgt. Alfredo González of Edinburg. This image shows Sol Marroquín on November 11, 1998. Sol and wife Blanca Marroquín are volunteers at the Mission Historical Museum.

Ismael "Kino" Flores was born (1958) and raised in La Joya. In 1977, he joined the U.S. Army and served three years at Fort Bliss, El Paso (shown in this undated photograph). Returning to the valley, he settled in Palmview. He later worked in Austin as a division manager for the Texas State Comptroller's Office. In 1996, voters of District 36 elected him to the Texas House of Representatives, where he still serves. He and his wife, Debra (Garcia), have two sons.

Lt. Gen. Derald Lary graduated from Mission High School in 1950 and from Baylor University in 1954. An officer in the U.S. Air Force for 35 years, he served in both command and management positions and accumulated over 4,000 flying hours. In South Vietnam, while operations officer for his squadron, he also flew 151 combat missions. Additional duty stations included Thailand, Japan, England, and Germany. In 1970, he earned an MBA from the University of Oklahoma, and he graduated from Air Force Command, from Staff College, and from the Royal College of Defense Studies in London. From July 1987 until his retirement in September 1989, Lieutenant General Lary was inspector general of the air force, concentrating on antiterrorism, counterintelligence, security inspections, flight and ground safety, and operational readiness. Throughout his career, he earned numerous awards and decorations. From 1990 until 2006, Lieutenant General Lary was director of aviation for the Miller International Airport in McAllen. He and his wife, Mary (Hoffer), are the parents of three children.

Juan J. Alanís, born in McAllen in 1949, grew up in Mission and graduated from Mission High School. Drafted into the U.S. Army in June 1969, he completed infantry and airborne training. Assigned to the 11th Cavalry (Black Horse), 2nd Squadron, E Troop, he shipped out to Vietnam. Alanís took part in search and destroy missions near the Cambodian border. Twice wounded in action (April 2, 1970, and October 10, 1970), Alanís was discharged on December 15, 1970. He received two Purple Heart awards and a Combat Infantry Badge for his service.

Virginia Bourbois (Cavazos) Silva joined the Texas Army National Guard (1978–1984). She was assigned to the 49th Armored Division, attached to the 3rd Battalion, 141st Infantry Division. An administrative specialist, she gained experience in financial and personnel matters. In 1990, she organized a support group for families of National Guard soldiers mobilized for Operation Desert Storm. In 1991, she became one of six state council members for Texas Family Support Groups under the Adjutant General's Office. She has received many commendations and lives in Mission with her husband, David, a retired army staff sergeant. More recent Mission service women include Margaret Ellen Turcotte (U.S. Army, 1998–2002), Spc. Lizette Ayde Salas (U.S. Army), and Alexandra Leal (U.S. Marine Corps).

Spc. Alex Daniel González (1987–2008) was born in McAllen and graduated from Mission High School, where he played football and baseball. He joined the U.S. Army in 2006 and was deployed to Mosul, Iraq, to serve in Operation Iraqi Freedom. Assigned to the 2nd Platoon, 43rd Combat Engineer Company, 3rd Armored Cavalry Regiment, he was a driver and gunner on the lead vehicle of the 2nd Platoon's route clearance patrols in Mosul. González received many awards, including the Bronze Star and Purple Heart.

Sgt. Javier Marín Jr. (1976–2005) of Mission enlisted in the U.S. Army in 1999. After basic training, he was assigned to the 2nd Battalion, 2nd Infantry Regiment, 1st Infantry Division, in Germany. He served as a rifleman, machine-gunner, Bradley Fighting Vehicle driver, unit armorer, grenadier, and infantry team leader. He was twice deployed to Kosovo (2002–2003). In 2004, he went to Iraq with Alpha Company, Task Force 82nd Engineers. He was killed when his Bradley Fighting Vehicle overturned northeast of Baghdad. Sergeant Marín received numerous awards, including the Bronze Star.

123

Spc. José Abraham Rubio-Hernández (1984–2008) was born and raised in Mission, where he graduated from Mission High School. He enlisted in the U.S. Army in 2006, and after training, he was assigned to Company A, Armored Battalion 4/64, and deployed to Baghdad, Iraq, where he commanded a Bradley Fighting Vehicle. Among his many awards were the Bronze Star and Purple Heart. He is survived by his wife and son.

S.Sgt. Omar Demetrio Flores (1978–2006) of Mission enlisted in the U.S. Army in 1996 and served until his death on July 8, 2006. He was stationed in Germany (130th Engineer Brigade) before his deployment to the Middle East with the 54th Engineer Battalion. Sergeant Flores, who supervised 30 soldiers and specialized in the deactivation of bombs, served two tours in Iraq. He was awarded numerous medals, including the Bronze Star and Purple Heart. He is survived by his wife and two children.

Spc. Edgar Adan Hernández was born in McAllen and graduated from Mission High School in 1999. In January 2000, he enlisted in the U.S. Army and received training as a logistics specialist. He deployed to Kuwait in February 2003 with the 507th Maintenance Company in support of the 5/52 Air Defense Brigade. Transferred to Iraq, he and his unit suffered heavy casualties during an attack by the Iraqi Republican Guard on March 23, 2003. Hernández and seven soldiers were captured and held in prisoner of war camps for 21 days. On April 13, 2003, U.S. Marines rescued Hernández and his fellow soldiers. Hernández reenlisted for four years, serving stateside, and received his discharge in June 2007. The recipient of many military awards and honors, Hernández is now a police officer with the Pharr, Texas, Police Department. He and his wife have two sons.

Sgt. José M. López (1910–2005) was born in Mission to parents originally from Oaxaca, Mexico. He grew up in Brownsville, where he enlisted in the U.S. Army. After landing at Normandy, France, on June 7, 1944, López and the 23rd Infantry, 2nd Infantry Division, pushed eastward. In Belgium on December 17, López held off Nazi tanks and infantry with a machine gun as Company K retreated to avoid being surrounded. His covering fire killed at least 100 of the enemy, gave Company K time to withdraw, and allowed supporting American forces to prevent Nazi advancement. López received the U.S. Congressional Medal of Honor as well as Mexico's highest honor, the Aztec Eagle. After the war, he remained in the army, serving in the Korean War, and retired as a master sergeant in 1973. He and wife Emilia (Herrera) were the parents of five children. Seen here in a parade to honor López during the Mission Citrus Fiesta, January 26–28, 2001, are, from left to right, officer Samuel Segura (Mission Police Department), Leo Peña (Mission City Council), Sergeant López, and Chief Leo Longoria (Mission Police Department).

BIBLIOGRAPHY

Barrera, Elena Farías. "Cayetano Barrera of La Reforma Ranch." *Rio Grande Roundup*. Mission, TX: Border Kingdom Press, 1980.

Boyle, Zac Drummond. "Drummond Family Live in Store after Arriving Here." The *Mission Times*. January 22, 1959.

Brunson, Jim. "La Lomita Historic District." *City of Mission Centennial Celebration Booklet*. Mission, TX: Mission Publishing Company, 2008: 16–18.

El Mesías United Methodist Church 90th Anniversary. Mission, TX: El Mesías United Methodist Church, 2002.

Heller, Dick D., Jr. *The History of Mission, Hidalgo County, TX*. Typescript, 1994 and 2003.

Kell Muñoz Architects. *La Lomita Mission Preservation Plan*. San Antonio, TX: self-published, 2007.

Ledvina, E. B., Rev. " 'Cavalry of Christ' a Band of Missionaries on Horses." *Extension Magazine*. April 1911. Reprinted in the *Mission Times*.

Lott, Virgil N. "First Settlers of Mission Named by Early Pioneer." The *Mission Times*. January 22, 1959.

———. "This I Remember." The *Mission Times*. January 22, 1959.

Norton, Robert L. "Moore Field." Typescript, 1980.

Olivarez, Kathy. "John J. Conway, Founder of Mission." *City of Mission Centennial Celebration Booklet*. Mission, TX: Mission Publishing Company, 2008: 26–28.

Richards, Althea Wright. "Wright Family Came to Mission in Early Days." The *Mission Times*. January 22, 1959.

Silva-Bewley, S. Zulema. *The Legacy of John H. Shary: Promotion and Land Development in Hidalgo County, South Texas 1912–1930*. Edinburg, TX: The University of Texas–Pan American Press, 2001.

Wallace, Lucy H. *In His Service Fifty Years, History of the First Presbyterian Church of Mission, Texas*. Mission, TX: First Presbyterian Church of Mission, 1960.

Watson, Mrs. James. *The Lower Rio Grande Valley of Texas, and Its Builders*. Mission, TX: The Lower Rio Grande Valley and Its Builders, Inc., 1931.

Wright, Robert, O.M.I. Southwestern Oblate Historical Archives, Oblate School of Theology, San Antonio, TX. Correspondence with Jim Brunson, *Progress Times News*, Mission, TX, August 19, 2008, by electronic mail.

Visit us at
arcadiapublishing.com

www.ingramcontent.com/pod-product-compliance
Lightning Source LLC
Chambersburg PA
CBHW050658110426
42813CB00007B/2043